COMING OF AGE
IN BOTSWANA

HEATHER ROSSER

With Happy memories

of our time in

Botswana

Heather (Rosser)

Published by New Generation Publishing in 2021

First Edition

ISBN
Paperback	978-1-80369-015-5
Ebook	978-1-80369-016-2

www.newgeneration-publishing.com

 New Generation Publishing

FOR

Adrian
Our daughters: Melinda, Emily and Alyrene
And our friends from Botswana

With thanks to Oxford Writers Group
for their support and encouragement

CONTENTS

Foreword

Coming of Age in Botswana is a sequel to Growing up in the Mandara Mountains which describes life in North East Nigeria in the early nineteen seventies.

Africa called us back and, in 1979, we arrived in Botswana where we lived for six eventful years. By the time we left Botswana we had three daughters, many life-long friends and a wealth of new experiences.

Although this book is a personal memoir, I have given context to our lives by mentioning world events when appropriate. We were fortunate to visit other African countries including Zimbabwe, South Africa, Swaziland, Kenya and, later, Namibia.

Our first 15 months was spent in Mochudi, near the capital, Gaborone. Adrian worked with the In-service Teacher Training team in primary schools and I worked in a Day Care Centre for pre-school children.

In 1980 Adrian was transferred to run the Teaching Aid Production Unit in Francistown which entailed running courses throughout Botswana. I had a variety of jobs including working for the Curriculum Development Panel and later as a journalist for the Botswana Guardian.

We returned to England in 1985 but kept our links with Botswana including a memorable trip back in 2005.

While I was writing this book forty years later I was amazed at the distances we had travelled on bush roads, often with our young children. We witnessed Botswana's magnificent wildlife, had numerous breakdowns in remote areas and encountered wonderful people along the way. Botswana has changed enormously since then but remains a land free from conflict where people have freedom of speech and live in peace with each other and the rest of the world.

Botswana means Land of the Tswana who are the largest ethnic group in Botswana.

Batswana refers to the people of Botswana.

Motswana is the singular of Batswana.

Setswana, usually known as Tswana, is one of the two official languages of Botswana, the other is English.

Botswana and Surrounding Countries

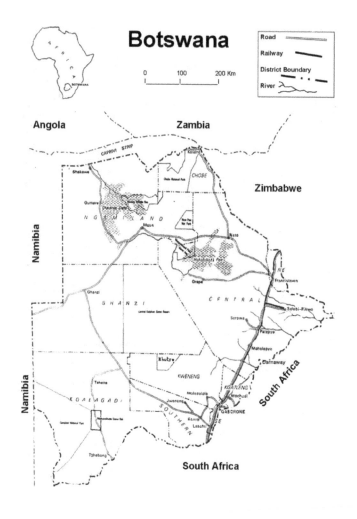

Trips around Zimbabwe

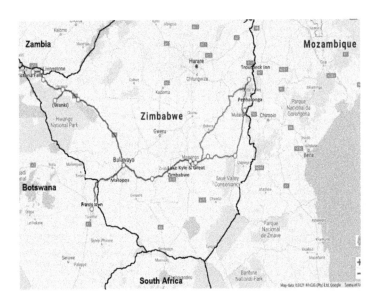

Trip around Ngamiland to Tsodilo Hills and Gcwihaba Caves.

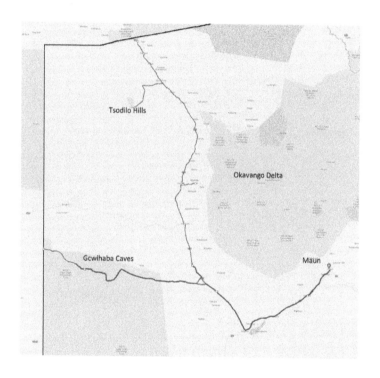

Trip home via Germany and Scandinavia

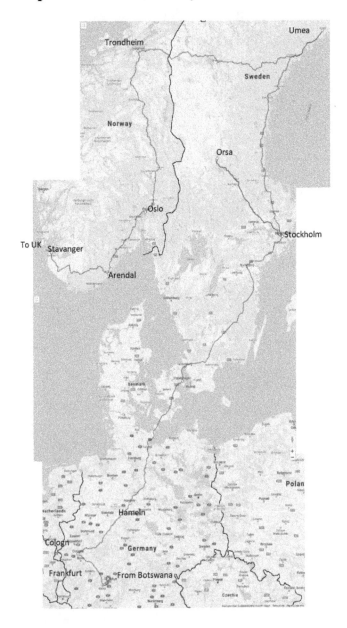

Part 1
Mochudi

Trip to Khutse Game Reserve

Chapter 1

Jan 1979
From Blizzard to Drought

'It's snowing!' Melinda announced excitedly as she ran into our bedroom followed closely by 18-month old Emily.

'Looks like it snowed all night.' I shivered as I opened the curtains to look at my parents' Somerset garden with its carpet of white.

'We'll be basking in the African sunshine tomorrow,' said Adrian cheerfully as he held up Emily to get a better view of the snow-covered trees and hedges.

'I've put out warm clothes for the journey to Heathrow and we can change when we get to Johannesburg.' I hoped I sounded positive about the long journey ahead and there wouldn't be any delays along the way.

My parents were determinedly cheerful when we sat down to breakfast.

'A Happy New Year!' My father raised his tea cup.

'It's only 11 months till we visit you,' said my mother stoically.

'It will be your second Christmas in Africa, although don't expect Botswana to be like Nigeria.'

I smiled as I remembered their interest in everything during their time with us in North East Nigeria when the country was still optimistic about its future.

'Melinda will be five next time we see her.'

'And me!' shouted Emily.

'Yes, you'll be two and a half.' My father looked fondly at his granddaughters then frowned and turned the radio up to hear the weather forecast.

'That doesn't sound good, you'll have to take it steady till you get to the motorway. It's a good thing you're not driving down from Market Rasen.'

I nodded and thought of our little cottage in the Lincolnshire Wolds. It would be more than two years before we saw it again.

An hour later we were ready to go.

Adrian inched the hire car carefully out of the drive as the girls waved frantically to their grandparents.

'It's a good thing we know our way,' I said as we went slowly past a signpost covered in snow.

'I think we're nearly at the motorway, we'll be able to speed up then.'

'I'm not so sure of that' I replied quietly.

As we drove down the slip road we saw that only one lane was open.

It was almost dark by the time we arrived at the British Airways terminal only to be told that all flights were cancelled.

'What, all of them!' I gasped.

Sensing the tension, Emily started to whimper and hugged her teddy bear closer.

'Where's our plane?' asked Melinda staring upwards.

'Daddy's finding out,' I said and turned to listen to Adrian asking what arrangements had been made.

'There will be no flights for five days,' the man at the desk told us impassively.

'But what will we do?' I shrilled as other passengers jostled behind us.

'Go home,' said the man with a shrug.

Adrian and I looked at each other in horror. Our tenants would already be installed in our house.

As we walked away I felt a tap on my shoulder. 'You could try South African Airways,' said a woman with an accent I was soon to become familiar with.

We joined a long queue and an hour later were hit by a blast of cold air as we walked the short distance from the South African Airways departure area to the plane, taking care not to slip on the slushy surface. It was eerily quiet and I realised there were no planes landing or taking off.

Relieved to be on the plane we settled into our three seats with Emily curled up on my lap. From his seat by the window Adrian gave me a running commentary of the pilot's efforts to manoeuvre our plane over the icy tarmac. After a couple of attempts the engines roared but we remained stationary.

'Ingenious!' said Adrian as he watched blasts of hot air from the engines directed downward and gradually melt the snow.

Very slowly our plane veered towards the silent runway, the engines gave a final roar and we were airborne.

12 hours later we touched down in Johannesburg.

When I was at University I had written a short dissertation on apartheid in South Africa as part of my sociology degree. Since then I had spent four happy years in Nigeria and I was ill-prepared for the reality of being in a police state even though we were only in transit. Despite everything running more efficiently than the chaos we had experienced at Heathrow I felt ill at ease during our short time in the airport and I kept a close eye on Melinda, fearful that she might speak out of turn in her excitement and apprehension about our new life ahead.

I was relieved when, several hours later, we boarded a small plane bound for Gaborone, the capital of Botswana. The girls were wide awake and Melinda was full of questions about where we were going to live and the friends she would make.

January is high summer in the southern hemisphere but as we neared Botswana the verdant countryside of South African gave way to a starker, more arid landscape. Every now and again we could see a small settlement but the population of Botswana in 1979 was less than a million and the villages were few and far between.

As the plane began its descent there was a sudden crosswind and I began to feel decidedly queasy.

'It's okay,' I muttered to Emily when she gave me a worried look.

The wheels hit the tarmac with a clunk and the plane was propelled forward before coming to an abrupt halt.

As we got off the air-conditioned aircraft I felt overwhelmed by the heat and screwed up my eyes against the sun's glare. We trailed behind the other passengers heading towards a small building with a corrugated roof in the distance which turned out to be the airport terminal. Fortunately, immigration and customs were cleared quickly and a couple in their late 50's came to great us.

'Bram Swallow,' said Adrian's new boss as he shook hands firmly. 'Welcome to Botswana'.

His wife stepped forward with her hand outstretched. She smiled at the children and looked at me sympathetically. 'You've had a long journey'.

I nodded mutely and promptly threw up at her feet.

Mortified by the manner of my greeting I shuffled across the car park and climbed into Mr Swallow's government Land Rover.

'I've booked you into the Holiday Inn for the next four nights, it will give you time to deal with the necessary formalities, get to know Gaborone and become acclimatised.'

Ten minutes later Mr Swallow helped us unload the luggage, gave Adrian instructions on how to get to his office next morning and drove off.

The girls showed their delight with our room by jumping on the beds. I looked out of the window at some children enjoying themselves in the play area. The lawn was a contrast to the parched hills beyond. Sitting in the shade of umbrellas the adults were enjoying their sundowner drinks.

'Well, here we are!' said Adrian. 'You'll be able to rest up for a few days while I sort out the paperwork and we get to know our way around Gaborone.'

I felt myself relax. 'Sounds good to me. Come on girls, you can have a quick shower and then we'll go down and find something to eat.'

The restaurant staff were used to children and a high chair was brought for Emily. There was something for all our tastes on the menu and when we had finished we retired to our room, relieved that we had a few days to recover from the upheaval of packing up our house, saying goodbye to family and friends and travelling from winter to summer.

I don't know when I'll be back,' said Adrian the following morning as he hailed a taxi to take him to the government area of Gaborone.

'We'll be fine, you're looking forward to playing outside aren't you?' I smiled down at Emily who looked a bit nonplussed as Adrian drove away.

We went back through the hotel and out to the play area. Melinda rushed ahead and was already on one of the swings when we caught up with her.

As I've discovered, time passes quickly for children when they are having fun but often tediously slowly for the parent in charge. I was relieved when I was joined by a couple of mothers and their children.

Unlike me, they lived in Gaborone and said they often brought their children to play here in the school holidays. They were shocked when I said we were going to live in Mochudi.

'Are there any other white families there?' asked the taller woman examining her polished nails.

Her friend appeared embarrassed. 'I expect there are some ex-pat teachers at the secondary school,' she said then added, 'Are you a teacher?'

'Yes, we both taught in Nigeria but my husband's job here is In-service Teacher Training, he'll visit primary schools and run courses for teachers.'

'Will he have to travel away for his work?'

'I don't know much about it, we were originally going to a Teacher Training College in Kenya but that fell through and so now we are here!'

'Will you be living in a government house?'

'I believe so, I'll find out later when my husband gets back.'

As the morning progressed there was a steady flow of women and children whiling away the time until the holidays were over.

They began to drift away around lunch time and we went into the restaurant for something to eat. We had just finished when Adrian appeared.

'I didn't expect you to be back so soon, is everything okay?'

'Amazing, I got everything done; would you like to go and choose a car this afternoon?'

We wanted a car that would be suitable for camping trips so we chose a Nomad van. The finance took a long time to raise and unfortunately it wasn't ready for delivery until February. Adrian had the use of a government Land Rover for work but private use was forbidden. We had been told that there was no supermarket in Mochudi so we stocked up on food supplies before we left.

It felt good to be on our way as we piled into the Land Rover and drove 38 km north to Pilane Junction. We crossed the railway line where the daily train stopped on its way from Johannesburg to Bulawayo in what was then called Rhodesia.

From there we turned east, taking care to avoid people and donkeys. Ten minutes later we arrived in Mochudi.

Chapter 2

Mochudi Welcome, Kgotla and Museum

As we arrived on the outskirts of Mochudi we saw a sign to the Government Offices. We turned off the road and parked outside a small single story building.

'Is this our house?' asked Melinda.

I shook my head, 'We'll be there soon.'

I held both children's hands as we walked towards the building. The Area Education Officer welcomed us formally. He handed Adrian a key to our house and a junior officer was delegated to take us there. It was, in fact, just round the corner in the Government Housing area.

The track was bumpy and covered by compacted sand. Our house was one of two large white-washed bungalows opposite a cluster of smaller houses. There was an expanse of dry grass behind the house and behind that a white building surrounded by a high wire fence which we learnt afterwards was the prison.

We parked in front of the garage and I noticed several thorn trees bringing shade to garden. The government officer checked that the keys were in order then left.

Inside, the house was spacious with a large sitting/dining room, three bedrooms and a bathroom. But it obviously hadn't been cleaned since the previous occupants.

Unaware of our shock at the dirt, the girls kicked off their shoes and ran round the outside of the house.

'Mind the thorns,' I warned.

We were wondering where to start when we heard footsteps and a cautious voice saying 'Dumela'.

'I'm Mmatsela,' said a women in her late twenties. 'My husband heard that an English family were arriving this week.'

We introduced ourselves and explained our immediate problem.

'These people! They give our country a bad name. I will get some things to help. I live just there.'

She pointed to the house diagonally opposite and hurried off.

After carrying a load of boxes into the kitchen I suggested we stopped for a cup of tea.'

'We're lucky the gas cylinder isn't empty,' said Adrian as I filled the kettle.

I gave the girls some orange squash and when Mmatsela returned we sat on the veranda with our tea. She told us that her husband, Hugh, was English and he worked for the Land Department based next to the Government office we had just been to.

'But now we must make your house comfortable,' she said.

I had nearly finished preparing the bedrooms when I heard children's voices and went to see who the newcomers were.

Mmatsela introduced her 11 year old daughter, Veronica, and her six year old niece, Tanasa. She handed Veronica a cloth and asked her to help clean the living room while Tanasa played outside with Melinda and Emily.

Around five o'clock several people greeted us as they walked past our house on their way home from work.

'I heard you'd arrived! I'm Hugh'.

A friendly looking Englishman came through our open gate carrying two bottles of beer. 'I thought you might be thirsty', he added as he handed them to Adrian.

We sat on the veranda chatting for a while and they invited us for supper the following day.

It was getting dark when they left. I went to switch on the light inside the house but nothing happened.

'There's no electricity,' I called to Adrian after I tried all the switches.

He looked around. 'The power must have been switched off, have we got a torch handy?'

'We'll just have to go to bed early.'

I felt suddenly very tired as I located the torch and candles then sorted out some food.

Fortunately, the girls were excited about sleeping in their new home and we all had an early night.

It was pitch dark when I woke to a terrifying sound, something between a shriek and a roar. I lay rigid, wondering what murderous practice was happening. Adrian switched on the torch. As he got up to investigate I realised the noise was coming from the direction of the prison. When he opened the curtain slightly the sound was louder. Then we heard a snorting noise and a mournful whinny. Adrian gave a relieved laugh and beckoned me to join him. Standing in the middle of the grass separating us from the prison was a donkey!

I breathed a sigh of relief and crept along the passage to see if it had disturbed the girls but they were fast asleep with their arms around each other. We went back to bed and slept fitfully until dawn broke.

The sound of the girls' pattering feet hailed our first full day in Mochudi.

After breakfast Adrian went to the Government Office in the hope of getting our electricity re-connected.

As I watched him walk away I wondered what life would be like for myself and the girls during the days ahead.

Just then a tortoiseshell cat appeared. It looked at us warily then rubbed against my leg.

'Cat!' shouted Emily and, with hands outstretched, toddled towards it.

The cat backed away as far as the open gate where it sat and stared at us.

'It's hungry,' said Melinda. 'It wants breakfast.'

When Adrian returned with a man from the electricity department the cat was preening itself having drunk a saucer of milk.

He raised his eyebrows, 'Don't let the girls touch it, you don't know where it's been.'

I nodded in agreement but we both knew we were fighting a losing battle.

The electricity meter was soon located and the man re-connected the supply.

We continued our unpacking until Melinda demanded to know what we were going to do next.

'Cat gone!' Emily said plaintively.

'Let's look round the town,' said Adrian. 'I know I'm only supposed to use the Land Rover for work but we need to find our way round Mochudi and see what shops there are.'

'It might even be market day,' I said.

Half an hour later we were driving down the bumpy track opposite our house to the main road. There was a group of people chatting outside a small off licence, or bottle store as we learnt to call it. The road continued downhill with houses scattered on either side, some thatched, some made of tin and others white-washed.

'We must be near the centre now.' I pointed to a sign saying library and next to that a small bank.

A little further on there were some single-story buildings which looked like government offices. Several had cars parked outside. There were a few round huts nearby which we later found were called rondavals.

Adrian parked next to a small general store.

As we got out I felt the hot sand through my sandals and it was a relief to be in the dim interior of the shop, although the two ceiling fans did little to mitigate the heat.

Most of the goods were brought in from South Africa and we were able to buy a few basic things we had forgotten in Gaborone.

'Where's the market?' I asked when we had paid for our goods.

'Market?' The shop assistant looked puzzled.

'Maybe there's only a market once a week,' Adrian said quietly.

'Okay.' I smiled at the assistant. 'When's market day?'

'We have no markets here,' he said.

'No markets in Botswana?' I looked at him in disbelief. He nodded. 'No markets.'

I couldn't believe it. Whenever we had visited even very small towns in Nigeria we had always found a market. Market day itself was always special with colourful displays of goods, people calling and holding up their wares and sometimes there was even singing and dancing.

'What's a market?' demanded Melinda.

'You remember where we sometimes met Granny and Papa in Market Rasen and we bought vegetables?'

'And went to the pub!'

'I smiled at my daughter. 'Yes, sometimes we went to the pub with them afterwards.'

Adrian put his hand on my shoulder. 'Let's put these things in the car then we can drive and see the rest of Mochudi.'

Unlike Nigeria, most of the people we passed, including the children, were wearing western clothes. A couple of motor cycles zoomed past, only to halt a few yards later when we came to the centre of the village. Ahead of us was a large open-sided building with a thatched roof.

'It looks like a meeting place', I said.

We got out of the Land Rover and were greeted by an elderly man. 'Have you come to visit the Kgotla?' he asked politely.

When we looked puzzled he said that the building we were standing by was the Kgotla, the community council and traditional law court.

'We are not like central government,' he said gravely, 'our decisions are always made by consensus'.

'That sounds truly democratic,' said Adrian before explaining that we had just arrived and he would be working with schools in the area.

'You must introduce yourself to Chief Linchway. He is away at the moment but he takes a great interest in education. I think this your first time in Botswana?'

'Yes, we arrived a few days ago,' I said.

'You will like living here, it is not hot like the Kalahari and there are some interesting hills to climb.' He turned and pointed, 'That is Phuthadikobo Hill and we have a museum at the top.'

'Can we go there now?' asked Melinda.

'I think it's time to go back to our house, we still have lots of unpacking to do'. We thanked the man and got back into the Land Rover.

I was feeling more optimistic by the time we arrived at our house, especially when I heard children's voices as we got out of the car.

A girl a bit older than Melinda and a boy about Emily's age were playing in the yard of the house opposite ours. They came to the fence and looked at us.

'Dumela!' I used the traditional greeting.

'Dumela, Mma.'

As was the custom, the girl looked at the ground making no eye contact with me as she answered, 'How are you?'

'We are well thank you. This is Melinda and this is Emily.'

'And this is our house, would you like to play?' Melinda jumped up and down excitedly.

The girl hesitated then, looking directly at Melinda, said, 'My name is Itulmeling and this is my brother.' She took his hand, 'Come Tumo, let's play.'

Led by Melinda the children ran up the veranda steps to the house.

'Sorry kids, you'll have to stay outside until we've unpacked,' I said firmly. 'I'll bring you some drinks when I've put the shopping away.'

Hugh had told us that the tap water in these government houses was safe to drink which was a relief after the bother we had in Nigeria with boiling and filtering it. I poured myself a glass and quickly tidied the kitchen.

The children were drawing pictures in the sand when I went outside with orange juice and biscuits. I was greeted by a pleasant looking woman standing by the gate. She introduced herself as Mrs Motsewole, the children's mother. She welcomed us and explained that her husband worked as a prison officer. I invited her to join us but she declined and, after telling her children to behave, Mrs Motsewole left to pound corn meal for later.

In the middle of the afternoon we had another visitor. He was in his mid-thirties, tall and with a mass of wavy hair.

'Hello, I'm Ted', he said. 'I expect Bram told you we'll be working together.'

Then, seeing the girls, he bent down and gravely shook their hands. For the next 15 months Ted was very much part of our lives, both as a colleague and friend.

On Mmatsela's recommendation I employed Bertha to help in the house. She was in her 20s, both friendly and efficient and Emily loved her, especially when she wrapped her on her back and carried her around while she was working. It was good to have her company the next morning when Ted took Adrian on a tour of the local primary schools which didn't open till the following week.

As they drove off, Itumeling and Tumo were standing at their gate and Melinda called to them to come and play. Their mother looked up from washing clothes in a tub.

'Dumela Mma', she said.

'Dumela, would the children like to play?'

Mrs Motsewole instructed them to behave themselves and the four children were soon playing like old friends.

When Adrian returned he told me that Bram was negotiating to use a room in the museum as a teacher's centre.

I said I would like to see it so, after lunch, we drove into Mochudi and parked at the bottom of Phuthadikobo Hill.

'There it is.' Adrian pointed to the building we had seen on top of the hill the previous day. 'Apparently it used to be the Mochudi National School until they moved to bigger premises.'

He hoisted Emily on his shoulder and we clambered up the steep steps to the top.

'What an amazing view!'

Winding across the plain was the Notwane River with small farms dotted about. On the other side we could see the hill behind our house.

At that moment a man came out of the museum.

'Hello! I see you've brought the family this time.' He shook my hand, 'I'm Sandy Grant, welcome to Mochudi.'

He told us that the museum had only been open four years but there was a steady flow of locals and visitors who wanted to explore the cultural heritage of the local Bakgatla tribe. Over the next 15 months we enjoyed regular walks up the hill and, once permission had been given for the Teachers Centre, the museum became Adrian's place of work.

We spent the rest of the week becoming acclimatised. Despite our previous experiences in West Africa, the intense heat was a shock. This was a dry heat which made us cough and the smell of dust pervaded the nostrils.

However, the girls were generally happy playing outside especially when the ginger cat appeared.

Adrian attached an old tire to one of our trees which all the children enjoyed swinging on. Later he fixed a bar between two of the trees for Melinda to swing and even hang upside down on.

As well as the Motsewole children, Poppy and her older sister, Cecilia, often dropped in to play. Their father drove a small bus and one of the highlights of the day for all the children was running down the lane at 5 o'clock when he parked outside their house. Occasionally he would let them clamber on board and he would rev the engine to their squeals of delight. Emily was so enamoured that she invented her own bus and a man to drive it.

Chapter 3

Friends at the Day Care Centre

I was beginning to settle into a routine and enjoyed hearing the children's laughter as they played together. However, this changed with the beginning of term the following week. Adrian and Ted were visiting schools and everything seemed uncannily quiet without the comings and goings of the neighbours' children.

'Can we watch Mr Benn?' asked Melinda.

I was surprised as it was the first time she had mentioned television. At home I had punctuated the day with various children's programmes. There were also visits to friends and to Market Rasen, often calling on Granny and Papa afterwards.

I looked at my watch; it was too early to call on Mmatsela.

'Let's do some painting.'

When I located the paint box I saw that I had forgotten to pack brushes but the girls were delighted when I suggested they use their fingers. They were soon busy daubing paint on some paper packaging I had kept. I got myself a glass of water and sat on the steps watching them enjoy the freedom of sticking their fingers in the paint.

'Nthuse!' exclaimed Bertha in amazement when she came out with the washing and stared at the children's paint stained hands.

'They've been having fun,' I said half apologetically. 'I think that's enough now girls. I'll put your paintings outside to dry, can you find some stones to stop them blowing away.'

When the girls were clean I suggested we call on Mmatsela.

'And play with Tanasa!' said Melinda.

'I'm sorry, she's at school today, why don't you take your doll with you.'

As always, Mmatsela was pleased to see us.

She asked about our life in England.

'It's hard when children can't see their grandparents,' she said sympathetically.

I told her that I used to help out at a local play group which Melinda and Emily enjoyed attending two mornings a week.

'There is a group like that here. It is known as crèche but I think the official name is Mochudi Day Care Centre. It is run by the YWCA. Do you have that organisation in your country?'

'Young Women's Christian Association? Yes but I don't know much about it.'

'They do good work for women. I think the one in Mochudi was started by teachers and nurses who want somewhere for their children to go when they are at work.'

'That's interesting. Where is it?'

'They have a building on this side of town. It is next to the road and is easy to see because there are swings outside.'

'Do you know who's in charge?'

Mmatsela shook her head. 'Why don't you go and see them, there might be some expat children from the secondary school.'

'That sounds great. We can go tomorrow.'

Melinda was excited when I said we would be going to play group the next day. I put Emily in the push chair and Melinda skipped along beside. However, after a while she became tired and so she stood on the foot rest and, as it was downhill, we bowled along. Fifteen minutes later we stopped at a notice saying Day Care Centre. Set in about one third of an acre were two low buildings and we could hear children's voices coming from the largest. We went to the open door and peered in.

There was a hush as all the children turned to look at us. Only one person seemed to be in charge and she came to greet us with a shy smile.

'Dumela Mma. Does your daughter want to come to crèche?'

I hesitated as I looked around the room. There were about fifteen nicely dressed children. Some were sitting at tables with paper and pencils while others were playing on the floor with roughly made building blocks. I couldn't see any toys or books.

The woman looked down at Melinda. 'I am Miss Kgobe. What is your name?'

Melinda told her and Miss Kgobe said, 'Children, say good morning to Melinda.'

A couple of the bigger girls smiled encouragingly as they repeated her name. However, I was taken aback when Miss Kgobe asked if Melinda would like to start immediately. She explained that crèche was open all day; the children had dinner together and then an afternoon sleep.

I wasn't sure but, impressed with the idea of having dinner followed by a sleep with the other children, Melinda begged me to let her stay.

It was with some misgivings that I left her and walked back up the hill with Emily.

I was hot and tired by the time we arrived at our house and Emily and I fell asleep after lunch.

I woke with a start and, after a quick drink of cold water, I put Emily in the push chair and set off briskly back to crèche.

Most of the children had already left when I arrived and I looked round anxiously for Melinda.

'Mrs Hersey took her', said Miss Kgobe.

I felt my stomach lurch. 'Who is she?' I asked as calmly as I could.

'She is a teacher, she is on the YWCA committee.'

'But why did she take her?' I felt my voice rise.

Miss Kgobe looked contrite. 'Melinda was crying. Mrs Hersey said she would take her to her house.'

Sensing my agitation Emily began to cry.

'The house is near. Come to the gate, I will show you.'

The remaining children followed us and waved as we left.

As directed, I turned off the road and walked past some rondavals till I came to slightly bigger houses with tin roofs. There was a little garden in front of one of them and I breathed a sigh of relief to see Melinda chatting to a pleasant looking woman weeding the flower bed.

'Minna!' Emily called happily when she saw her sister.

The woman stood up. 'Ah Mma Melinda, I am Mrs Hersey. I am a teacher and also on the crèche committee. My classes finished early today so I went to visit crèche and found Melinda looking sad so I brought her to my house. We had a nice cool drink together didn't we Melinda?'

'There was only water at crèche and it wasn't cold,' said Melinda mournfully.

Mrs Hersey told me with some pride that she had her own fridge.

'Thank you so much, I shouldn't have left Melinda all day.'

'Perhaps she can just come in the morning; her sister can come too. Would you like that?' she asked Emily who nodded vigorously.

I wasn't sure. 'Would you like to go in the mornings?' I looked at Melinda.

'They wanted to touch my hair,' she whispered.

'That's because you have such lovely blonde hair,' Mrs Hersey smiled sympathetically.

'Emily is too young to be left on her own,' I said firmly.

'Then you can stay with her.' Mrs Hersey looked at me shrewdly and added 'Are you a teacher?'

'Yes but…' I was going to say that I had no experience of teaching small children but, having taught at a Teacher Training College in Nigeria and been a regular helper at Melinda's play group in Lincolnshire, I was probably better qualified than the overworked Miss Kgobe. And anyway, how else were we going to occupy our days?

'Ok, we will come every morning and go home at lunch time.'

Mrs Hersey beamed. 'I will tell the committee, they will be very pleased. Now let me give you a cool drink before you leave.'

As we sat outside her house she greeted people as they passed. Some were carrying shopping bags on their heads and some were children skipping along in yellow and brown uniforms. Several people wanted to be introduced to us and they welcomed us to Mochudi.

Mrs Hersey told me that her husband was English and worked for the highways department.

I asked if she had been to England and she shook her head. 'Sometime we will go but we have our jobs and I am busy with YWCA.'

Feeling refreshed, I said goodbye and began the mile walk uphill; it was exhausting and I began counting the days till our car would be ready.

Melinda and Emily ran to play with the other children as soon as we arrived back home and Adrian and Ted returned soon afterwards.

It was interesting listening to them talk about their day and their plans for running more teachers' courses and Adrian was pleased that I had somewhere to take the girls and keep me busy.

When we arrived at crèche the next day some of the children clapped and Miss Kgobe looked relieved especially when I told her that I planned to help every morning.

In fact, I was left in charge and was shocked to see that Miss Kgobe was responsible for cooking the food as well as looking after the children. I later found out that, due to the drought, Botswana received aid from the UN World Food Programme. All schools received a regular supply of 50 kilo bags containing high protein powdered cereal with added vitamins. Each morning and dinner time a sufficient amount was cooked for the children.

I found some crayons, paper and a few pairs of scissors in one of the cupboards. When they got tired of drawing and cutting I taught them to sing 'Here we go Round the

Mulberry Bush' and a few other songs that Melinda had learnt at her play group.

The next morning we had a visitor. She had a friendly smile and introduced herself as Nora, a Zambian who did the accounts for the Apprentice Mechanics Brigade next door to crèche. She explained that her husband taught English at the Secondary School and they had a daughter called Tina who was about the same age as Melinda.

Nora greeted the children who were sitting at the tables eating their breakfast.

They answered politely and one little girl added 'Dumela Mma Tina.'

'Dumela Amelia,' smiled Nora.

'Amelia is from Rhodesia, her father teaches History at the Secondary School and her mother is a primary school teacher.'

She added quietly, 'They are Shona and have fled from the war there.'

'It has been going on a long time,' I said. I was going to add that my mother had a friend who lived in Bulawayo but I realised that it would be inappropriate as she and her husband had been given their land by the British Government after the Second World War. Understandably the indigenous population were demanding it back.

The following morning Nora dropped Tina at crèche. When she heard that I didn't have a car she volunteered to drive us home each day until ours was ready.

Nora and I got on well and a few days later she invited us to visit them at the Secondary School on Sunday afternoon.

We were still waiting for our car and Adrian was a bit worried about taking us in the government vehicle but Ted said it would be fine as it was technically a school visit!

The school was beautifully situated on the side of Phuthadikobo Hill. Unlike the government houses where we lived, the gardens were well established with flower beds including purple hibiscus and bougainvillea as well as several varieties of trees.

Michael was English and had met Nora when he was teaching in the west of Zambia. While the children played we spent the next hour exchanging African experiences. The girls were persuaded to sit still when Nora brought tea and cake. Conversation turned to the crèche and Michael said that there were several ex-pat families as well the Rhodesians who might be interested in their children attending. He suggested that we apply to international organisations for funding.

Our life began to take on a pattern. Officially Adrian started work at 7.30 but, unless he was visiting one of the more remote schools, he didn't leave his office in our garage till later.

Melinda, Emily and I used to arrive at the day care centre at about 9.30. One morning a smartly dressed woman arrived at the centre as the children were sticking pictures I had cut from magazines using flour and water paste. She introduced herself as the Chairman of the YWCA and said that Mrs Hersey had told the committee about me. She was impressed to find the children busy and asked if there was anything I needed for the crèche.

'Another teacher,' I said without hesitation.

'Oh!' This was obviously something the committee hadn't considered. 'I thought you were going to say more equipment'.

'That would be good too but Miss Kgobe has no time to teach as well as doing all the cooking.'

She glanced outside where Miss Kgobe was scrubbing the cooking pots and said she would discuss it with the committee.

Two weeks later I met Mrs Beatrice Ketley, a large motherly woman who the committee had decided to employ at the centre, allowing her to bring her three year old twins. She was older than Miss Kgobe who appeared relieved rather than offended when Mrs Ketley took charge. As time passed Beatrice and I became good friends and the children got on well together.

She told me that her husband, like many Batswana men, worked in the mines in Johannesburg and only returned for Christmas. As I met more women in Botswana I realised that their resilience and independence was partly due to having to manage on their own.

With Beatrice and Miss Kgobe to keep the centre clean as well as sometimes helping with the activities I prepared, more people began to send their children.

Nora told friends of hers at the secondary school about the Day Care Centre and we became multinational with children from Ghana and Holland as well as Botswana, Rhodesia and Britain. Soon they were communicating in both Setswana and English

When I told Mary from Ghana that Adrian and I had spent a year teaching in Ghana she invited us for lunch. She and her husband, Botchway, wanted to know what we thought of their country which was going through a period of unrest since we were there in the late 1960s.

Mrs Hersey invited me to meet the committee and we discussed the possibility of applying for outside funding. I spent the next few months applying for a grant from USAID to spend on equipment.

In addition, Mary Murphy my friend from University, did some fundraising in her home town of Manchester and raised an incredible 400 pounds.

When Adrian was transferred to Francistown fifteen months later it was good to know that Mochudi Day Care Centre would continue to thrive.

Chapter 4

Matsiengs Footprints, Lady Mitchison and Tropic of Capricorn

Five weeks after arriving in Botswana we received a message saying that our Nomad car was ready. Ted took Adrian to Gaborone and we waited in anticipation for his return. He caused quite a stir when he drove up our bumpy lane in a white vehicle that looked a bit like a small Land Rover.

It felt good to be at the wheel the next day as I drove the girls to crèche. When we arrived all the children gathered round and marvelled at the strange looking car while Beatrice and Miss Kgobe gave their enthusiastic approval.

That Saturday we celebrated by driving to Gaborone with Hugh, Matsela, Veronica and Tanasa. Our first stop was the Club which was founded in 1965, a year before Botswana became independent. As well as a club house there were tennis courts, lawns, brightly coloured flower beds and a swimming pool. It felt like an oasis compared with the parched landscape we had driven through. It was midday and I wasn't surprised that we were the only ones in the pool. The girls enjoyed splashing about in the water and were reluctant to get out but we were worried about them getting sunburnt. However the promise of cool drinks and snacks at the club house enticed them out.

Afterwards we drove the short distance to the shopping mall and went our separate ways, agreeing to meet later at the President Hotel. We had brought our cool bag and ice packs which we filled with food we bought in the supermarket.

Next, we went to the well-stocked Botswana Book Centre. The girls were delighted to choose a book each and I stocked up on paint brushes, coloured pencils and other 'essentials'. There were a few international newspapers and magazines as well as the Government owned daily newspaper.

The President Hotel was cosmopolitan and we enjoyed sitting on the large balcony and watching people of all nationalities coming and going along the mall.

'Look, there's Tanasa!' shouted Melinda when she saw her friend skipping towards the hotel.

It was a treat for all of us to order cool drinks in these comfortable surroundings. However, when the girls started demanding afternoon tea we thought it was time to leave.

We had all got on so well that Hugh suggested we took a picnic to Matsieng's footprints the following day.

I awoke to the sound of singing. A group of women wearing their best clothes were clapping and singing as they passed on their way to one of the churches in town. For a moment I felt homesick as I thought back to the last time I had been to church was for the Christingle service in our village when the children had proudly carried their Christingle oranges and candles. I smiled as I remembered how the vicar had hurried through the service in his anxiety that the candles might set light to the little girls' hair. However, I knew that things had changed for my friends and neighbours as well as us. When we tuned into the World Service we heard about what was being called Britain's Winter of Discontent with strikes, inflation and the coldest winter for 16 years. In comparison, life here had lots to offer.

We had decided to make an early start so after a quick breakfast, I packed some food in the cool bag and we were ready to go. However, we were soon to learn that Hugh had a habit of being late but, as he always turned up smiling, he was usually forgiven.

As we drove north along the almost deserted A1 highway, Hugh and Mmatsela told us what they had heard about the footprints although at that time very little was known about the origins around Matsieng, the great hunter. According to the legend, Matsieng, a giant one-legged man, emerged from a waterhole. He was followed by his animals and his people. Then they strode off to settle the surrounding lands, leaving their footprints behind.

'I think we turn off here,' said Hugh after we had been going for about twenty minutes.

Adrian slowed down when we came to a sandy track to our right. 'This wouldn't be so easy in a saloon,' he said as he drove the Nomad over the ridges and pulled up at the end of the track.

In front of us was a raised area of sandstone rock with a few small pools breaking up the surface. We parked under a shady mopane tree and the girls began to clamber on the flat but uneven rocks, hunting for footprints.

'There's one!' said Veronica pointing to a carving of a single foot.

'Let's see!' Melinda had already kicked off her shoes and put one foot on the carving. 'It fits!' she shouted.

'It must be a child's footprint' said Adrian; 'Look there's some bigger ones over there.'

For the next half hour we scrambled among the rocks finding human and animal footprints of various sizes. Interestingly, none of them were in pairs.

'How old do you think they are?' I asked.

Hugh shook his head. 'No one seems to know anything about them.'

It was another 20 years before Botswana was to become a tourist destination and more research was done into these ancient rock carvings, or petroglyphs to give them the official name. It was found that there are over one hundred engravings possibly dating back ten thousand years. Their precise origin is still unknown but they are believed to have been created by early hunter gathers.

I sat on a rock, soaking up the heat and absorbing the timeless nature of the place. Two scarab beetles were struggling to roll a ball of dung several times their size up one of the rocks, their black shells iridescent in the hot sun. I had once played the part of Mrs Beetle in a school production of The Insect Play and, with Mr Beetle, had rolled a huge papier-mâché ball of imaginary dung around the stage so it was fascinating to see it happening in reality.

A whistling call made me look up. Perched high up on a tree was a goshawk, its red talons wrapped around an outermost branch. Wishing I had binoculars, I watched for several minutes until, disturbed by a shout from the children, it stretched its huge wings and glided silently away.

'I'm thirsty', announced Melinda and we all agreed it was time to sit in the shade and have our picnic.

'It is too hot,' said Mmatsela after we finished.

I agreed but the children didn't appear to notice the heat. Wishing that I could entice them with the promise of an ice cream, I suggested that they could explore for another fifteen minutes.

Unbothered by the heat, Adrian and Hugh found more footprints and animal tracks embedded in the rocks.

'Do you think this used to be a sacred place?' I asked Mmatsela.

She shrugged. 'I don't know but Botswana is a modern country now.'

I felt disappointed. After my research into customs in Nigeria, I had hoped to be able to do something similar in Botswana.

Perhaps she sensed my disappointment. 'Another time we must go to my cattle post. I think you will find it interesting.'

Thank you, that will be lovely.'

I knew it was the custom in Botswana for people to keep their cattle many miles from where they lived. Even now, cattle are essential to Botswana's economy but often the arid landscape means they have to graze over large areas.

At that moment two large brown cows came out of the bush and began lapping up water from one of the pools.

Emily cried and fell over in her rush to get away.

'Time to go kids!' said Adrian, scooping Emily up.

Ted called soon after we got back. He had heard that Naomi Mitchison was arriving in Mochudi in a few days and she wanted to see the work that he and Adrian were doing in the local schools.

While we sat in the shade Ted told us about Lady Mitchison who, in Botswana, held the title of Mother of the Bakgatla. She had met Linchway at a British Council party held to give newly arrived overseas students in Britain the opportunity to meet people. They kept in touch and he invited her to Botswana for his investiture as Chief of the Bakgatla tribe. From then on she visited Botswana almost every year and helped set up a school, the library and the museum.

'Where will we take her?' asked Adrian.

'She says she wants to visit the river schools,' said Ted doubtfully, 'but she's an old lady and they are eighty kilometres away on the border with South Africa.'

'What are the River Schools?' I asked.

'They are schools alongside the Limpopo River. There are two in the area, the furthest is at Oliphants Drift.'

'That's not far!' said Adrian.

'You haven't seen the road!'

'How old is she?' I asked.

'I heard someone say she's eighty. She's a very energetic woman; I believe she writes books as well.'

'She sounds interesting, and it will be an opportunity to get to know the schools in that area.' Adrian looked pleased at the prospect.

A few days later, Adrian and Ted left early to pick up Lady Mitchison and take her to the schools.

We had just finished lunch when they arrived back at our house.

She was wearing a long skirt and headscarf and was smaller than I expected. Her face was lined but her eyes were piercing.

When Adrian introduced her as Lady Mitchison she said, 'No, don't bother with that, I'm Naomi and you're Adrian.'

I could see that both Adrian and Ted were slightly taken aback when she said, 'Now where are we going this afternoon?'

Ted ran his fingers through his tousled hair. 'Well, perhaps a couple of the schools in town.'

I quickly made some sandwiches for them while Adrian, at her request, showed her his office in the garage.

'I like to see people using their initiative but it will be good when you have a proper teachers' centre in the museum, I'll see if I can put pressure on the powers that be to hurry that up,' Lady Mitchison said over lunch.

As they prepared to leave she pointed, to the letters ISTT on the Land Rover. 'What does that stand for?'

'In Service Teacher Training. It was set up to run workshops on how to teach the new curriculum,' said Adrian.

'But each school has different needs and we adapt our methods to suit each situation', added Ted and opened the passenger door.

'That's most important,' agreed Lady Mitchison as she leapt into the seat with remarkable agility.

When Adrian arrived home late in the afternoon it was the first time since we arrived that I had seen him looking quite so tired after a day's work.

After the girls had gone to bed we sat outside enjoying the cool of the evening and gazing at the stars. I asked Adrian about the river schools he had visited. He said that it was a similar situation to the primary schools in North-East Nigeria with the town schools having better facilities than those in remote areas.

He thought for a moment then added, 'We nearly got driven off the road by a sledge!'

I laughed in disbelief.

'Was it pulling a reindeer?'

'No, four oxen. They were coming towards us at quite a pace and we had to get off the road quickly which wasn't easy as it was deep sand.'

He went on to explain that the 'driver' was holding on to the reins and behind him were some sacks, presumably of food.

'Now that we've got the car you'll be able to see more of the area at weekends, though I think I'll leave any sandy tracks for a while!

The next weekend we headed north again past Matsieng's Footprints until we came to the Tropic of Capricorn.

We parked under a shady tree then posed for photos next to the sign. Although not really understanding, the girls caught our excitement as we took them from one side of the sign to the other, jumping in and out of the Tropics.

We had just finished having drinks and snacks from the cool box when a battered Toyota Hilux pickup pulled up and a friendly weather worn man in his 50s got out.

'Good Day to you,' he said in a South African accent. 'What brings you to the Tropic?'

We explained and he said that he was waiting to give someone a lift to one of the farms on the River Limpopo. He pointed to a sandy track opposite.

'Do people use sledges?' I asked.

'No, this is the Southern Tuli Block. All the farms belong to white farmers. We all have Land Rovers and tractors, much easier than a sledge, aye?' He smiled at the girls.

We chatted for a while until a lorry stopped and a young man jumped out.

'I'll be going then, have a good day,' the man said.

Little did any of us know that our brief exchange at the Tropic would lead to a friendship lasting many years.

Chapter 5

Apartheid, Mafeking and Soweto

Now that we had our own transport we looked forward to exploring and being able to go with Hugh and Mmatsela to the cattle post. However, it had to be postponed until Mmatsela was well enough following surgery in South Africa that was unavailable in Botswana.

They were slightly anxious about the reception they would get as in 1949 the South African Government had introduced the Prohibition of Mixed Marriages Act. However, they had no problems and on their return told us how fascinated the medical staff had been to see a mixed race couple and they kept coming to look at them. Both Hugh and Mmatsela had a natural charm and they were treated well both by the black staff and the Afrikaner doctors.

Apartheid in South Africa was complicated. White was the name for British and other Europeans settlers. Afrikaans or Boers were white settlers of Dutch origin, Boer being the Dutch word for farmer. Asians were migrants, many of Indian origin and involved in trading. Coloured referred to mixed black and white settlers. Black was the name given to black Africans; many of them had arrived around the same time as the Europeans but from areas north of South Africa. The indigenous population were despised by all groups and referred to as Bushmen and Hottentots; the Bushmen were sometimes even hunted for sport.

When Mmatsela was fully recovered she suggested that we spent a night at the cattle post and we agreed with enthusiasm.

'Did you bring a tent by any chance?' asked Hugh.

I shook my head. 'We were thinking it might be useful but we had a caravan at home so we didn't go camping.'

'I'll get one in Gaborone,' said Adrian. 'Bram wants to see me next week so I'll look then.'

'You can try but I doubt if you'll find one.'

As Hugh predicted, there were no tents in Gaborone but Bram had called Adrian to discuss a visit to Mafeking across the border in South Africa. He wanted to get a quote from a publisher there for school text books and suggested that Adrian could take us too. He knew that the job entailed a lot of travelling so he sometimes allowed family to go along especially, as in our case, the spouse was also a teacher.

At school I had learned about the Boer War which ended with the eight month siege of Mafeking in 1902. The British Colonel in charge of the garrison was Robert Baden-Powell who went on to found the Scout Movement.

In more recent history Mafeking had become the capital of the nominally independent territory of Bophuthatswana in 1977. It was a Homeland, or Bantustan, and was not recognised by any government except South Africa which continued to exert its control in all areas of life. Until 1994 it was one of four independent Bantustans but, with the end of apartheid after the first multi-racial elections, it ceased to exist and became part of South Africa again.

Melinda's excitement at travelling to another country was infectious and she and Emily busied themselves packing toys for the journey, most of which I surreptitiously removed later. When we arrived after a two and a half hour journey, we realised we should have made an earlier start as all the hotels were full. This made purchasing a tent essential and we were fortunate to get the only one in Mafeking as well as some foam mattresses.

The municipal camp site was pleasantly situated round a small lake which partly made up for our disappointment when we found out the tent was only big enough to accommodate myself and the girls.

'Don't worry, I'll sleep in the car', said Adrian.

I am still renowned for travelling with enough food to cope with a delay on any journey and, although we had been looking forward to treating ourselves to a meal out, I unpacked a picnic that was still edible having been in our large cold box.

'We must bring a table and folding chairs next time', I said as I put a blanket on the grass.

The girls were sleepy and, after our picnic, were content to sit quietly watching the red and gold hues of a stunning sunset. Silhouetted against its rays was a tree which appeared to be in full leaf.

'That's odd,' said Adrian, pointing to the tree. Suddenly there was a hoot from a train at the edge of the camp site and the 'leaves' turned into a flock of swallows flying above our heads before returning to roost on the tree.

'Look girls!' Adrian pointed upwards. 'See the birds, they are swallows getting ready to fly to England.'

'How do they know the way?' asked Melinda.

'That's a mystery. It's called migration; soon it will be winter here so they are going to England where it will be spring time. When they arrive they'll make a nest and lay eggs which will turn into baby swallows.'

'But England is far away.' Melinda looked at me in disbelief.

'It's true.' I said, 'they might even fly to Granny and Grandad's house!'

Sometimes Melinda was sad when we talked about her grandparents but on this occasion both she and Emily were excited about sleeping in the little tent and they were soon asleep.

'The Nomad will be a good place for star gazing', said Adrian as we sat looking at the night sky.

'I don't see how, unless you sit up all night.'

'I'll put a mattress on the roof'.

'Okay. Hope the stargazing is good.'

Adrian was still sound asleep when the girls woke up. They were unsurprised to see their father on the car roof and called him to join them as they ran about on the dew covered grass in their night clothes.

I wandered to the edge of the lake and was delighted to see a grey heron wading among the bulrushes. In the distance I heard the sound of bird song and suddenly hundreds of swallows were wheeling and circling overhead. Remembering our conversation the night before I took comfort in the thought that some of them might be heading for England.

Although we didn't know it then, swallows nested in the eaves of the house we bought on our return to Lincolnshire. From then on we have always considered them to be a special link with Africa.

Melinda didn't want to leave when we had taken down the tent.

'Can we come again with Mmatsela and Hugh? Tanasa would really like it here.'

Adrian and I looked at each other. 'They wouldn't be allowed', I said sadly.

'Why not? They are our friends!'

We explained as best we could but the situation defied reason.

'Would you like to have breakfast in the Wimpy Bar we saw yesterday?' I said weakly changing the subject.

Despite feeling unsettled by our conversation with Melinda, breakfast was a treat for us all. As we ate, I asked Adrian if he had seen any interesting stars from the car roof.

'The Southern Cross,' he said animatedly 'and the Plough was upside down! Do you remember, it was on its side when we saw it in Nigeria?'

'Vaguely', I said as I thought back to tropical nights in the Mandara Mountains.

Much to the girls' delight, he began to sketch the constellation on a napkin as he explained how it appeared different depending where in the world you were.

When we had finished, Adrian dropped us off at a large park with an open air swimming pool while he visited the publisher. Apart from two middle-aged South African women, we had the pool to ourselves which surprised me as we were in an allegedly independent state. The only black people were three cleaners, slowly and painstakingly keeping the area clean.

On his return, Adrian told us the publisher had suggested we drive back via Zeerust as it was a better road, presumably because it was in South Africa. The town was originally called Coetzee's Rust after the white settler who bought the land but it was later abbreviated to Zeerust.

We passed bungalows with neat gardens and then slowed down to stare at a magnificent baroque style building which turned out to be the railway station.

On our way out we stopped at a liquor store to buy beer and soft drinks to take back as we had heard that prices were cheaper in South Africa. There were two queues so Adrian went to the shortest. The young black man in front of him looked round nervously and shuffled forward. Suddenly a white man rushed out of the store shouting and pointing to signs above two different entrances, one saying Black and the other White.

Adrian seemed about to say something but thought better of it and joined the queue for whites.

'Car fast', commented Emily gleefully as, after Adrian had packed away the bottles, he revved the engine and drove quickly away.

The scenery was similar to Botswana with scrubby bush, a few trees and scattered villages but every now and again we would pass high gates which signalled the entrance to a large farm.

Botswana had an ambivalent relationship with South Africa. Many of the South Africans living in Botswana had originally arrived as refugees, mainly black but some were white opponents to the apartheid regime. However, Botswana was heavily dependent on the larger and more powerful nation for all sorts of goods, especially food.

During the next six years Adrian had several trips to South Africa on business, with the most interesting being a visit to Soweto. When we lived in Francistown in the north of Botswana, Adrian ran the Teaching Aid Production Unit, known as TAPU, which provided teaching aids, including books, to schools throughout Botswana. The Unit was asked by a Pastor in Soweto if they could provide relevant books for a primary school he was involved with. Adrian was intrigued but also slightly worried about going. Soweto was the largest of the townships which were created to provide housing for the mining industry and to control the influx of black people into one area. Houses were constructed from whatever material people could afford. Supplies of water and electricity were erratic and after the Soweto uprising in 1976 the townships were increasingly volatile.

Adrian travelled to Johannesburg with Hendrix, his Motswana driver who dropped him at a hotel. The Pastor had arranged for a local black driver to pick him up the following day as a Botswana Government vehicle in Soweto could arouse suspicion.

Feeling unsure of the reception he would get, Adrian walked across the playground. It was early and a group of teachers were standing talking.

'Good morning,' he said hesitantly and was shocked when everyone turned their backs on him.

Clutching his bag of books, he took a few steps forward and greeted the nearest person in Setswana.

'Dumela Ra. O tsogile jang?'

'Ke tsogile sentle', he replied automatically then looked at Adrian. 'Ke kopa tshwarelo! I am sorry, are you the speaker?'

'Yes, I'm from Francistown.'

'You are welcome.' He beckoned to the Pastor who hurried over to welcome the 'guest from Botswana'.

They went into the staff room where Adrian showed them some short books with black and white illustrations. These had all been written by Batswana teachers during workshops organised by TAPU throughout the country. He explained that they had been fortunate to get overseas funding for equipment to print the books which were met with approval as they were passed round.

Adrian answered questions about schools in Botswana but he was unable to say anything about the possibilities of leaving South Africa to work in Botswana. He knew several people who had, but he had heard of even more who had been killed or tortured as they tried to flee the regime.

He was shocked when, as he was leaving, the Pastor told him that all water and electricity in the township could be remotely switched off, with the exception of huge street lights which dominated the place and ensured that anyone on the streets at night could be seen.

By this time Nelson Mandela had been in prison for 22 years.

Adrian was pleased to see Hendrix waiting for him with the Land Rover outside the hotel. Even keeping within the business district of Johannesburg made them feel uncomfortable and they were both pleased when the purchase of printing equipment for TAPU was completed.

Chapter 6

Cattle Post and Khutse Game Reserve

We were keen to use our tent again and were delighted when Mmatsela and Hugh invited us to their cattle post.

I mentioned to Beatrice Ketley at crèche where we were going and she said that she would take us to her lands sometime. Unlike cattle posts, people's lands are nearer towns and for growing crops, not keeping livestock. She seemed surprised that Mmatsela had a cattle post because they were usually the preserve of the men while the lands were farmed by women. I explained that Matsela owned it jointly with her brother who worked in Gaborone and that they employed a boy who lived at the cattle post and looked after the cattle.

Her brother, Kwai, arrived on Saturday morning and helped load Hugh's truck with sorghum for the cattle boy and salt, pellets and vaccination kit for the cattle.

Melinda was excited about travelling in the back of the open truck with Adrian and Kwai. Mmatsela, Emily and I sat in front while Hugh drove. The roads were pure sand and after two hours of concentrated driving we stopped for a picnic. We were about to leave when we saw some deer-like creatures grazing near a clump of trees.

'Impala,' shouted Hugh but they took off, leaping gracefully into the long grass.

Once we were back in the car we kept a careful look out for more wildlife and were rewarded by seeing a large kudu with magnificent spiralled horns standing by the side of the road.

Driving became more difficult and I was pleased it wasn't me at the wheel.

'We are almost there,' said Mmatsela after another half hour. About a kilometre further on we arrived at our destination.

In front of us was a kraal for the cattle surrounded by a thick hedge of cut thorn bushes. There was also a lapa which was a larger enclosure with a kitchen area and a sleeping area. It had a roof held up by poles but there were no walls.

'The cattle boy has done a good job,' said Mmatsela as we looked at the well swept earth floor and spotlessly tidy area.

We unloaded the vehicles then went to the community borehole where we met the cattle boy. He was about 12 years old, barefoot and wearing khaki shorts and a faded t-shirt.

The borehole acted as a community centre for all the nearby cattle posts. It was owned by a syndicate of famers who paid for its installation and maintenance. The pump was powered by diesel so the escalating oil prices were beginning to cause problems.

On our return to the lapa, Mmatsela began to prepare the meal. Adrian put up the tent and then we went to collect firewood. The evening light filtering through the trees gave the place an air of tranquillity. When we had enough wood we returned to the lapa and Hugh lit a fire which we sat round and ate a traditional meal of sorghum porridge with meat and vegetables. The cattle boy brought some friends and they played their home-made guitars. One was made from a cooking oil tin, it had three strings and I was amazed at the melodious sound that came out of it. After a while the boys ran off into the bush, maybe to sit round someone else's fire.

I slept in the tent with the girls while Adrian was on a blanket outside. Mmatsela, Hugh and Kwai settled down by the fire for the night.

We were up early the next day as there was a lot to do. All the cows had to be rounded up and brought to the kraal then taken to the cattle crush near the bore hole to be vaccinated. Kwai and the cattle boy went to round up the cows while Hugh, Mmatsela and Adrian cut down thorn branches to strengthen the wall of the kraal. Melinda and Emily played happily in the lapa. Suddenly we heard loud mooing and shouting and saw clouds of dust as a herd of cows in different shades of brown came running towards the kraal followed by Kwai and several cattle boys waving sticks. The children and I sat in the truck for safety and also to get a good view. Although there were about forty cattle, only half of them belonged to Mmatsela and Kwai so they had to separate theirs. The cattle were of different shades of brown and to the casual onlooker there was little difference between them but Mmatsela and Kwai knew each of theirs individually. They went off again to find the rest of their cattle and the process started over again. By the time they were all rounded up there was a cacophony of sound coming from the kraal.

After lunch the men drove the cows to the cattle crush near the bore hole. We followed slowly and arrived just in time to take up ringside seats for the real drama. The cattle crush is a small fenced passage between two kraals. The cows wait in the larger kraal then about eight of them are forced into the cattle crush, one behind the other. Two farmers who had been taught how to give injections gave the vaccinations but it wasn't an easy task and one man vaccinated his hand. The air was filled with shouts of exasperation and angry mooing which Emily seemed to find highly amusing especially when the mooing was accompanied by splattering from the cows' bowels. One of the most difficult parts of the process was the timing in raising the pole at the end of the crush for the cows to go into the second kraal after their vaccination. It then had to be lowered quickly enough to stop the unvaccinated cows passing through. One cow did manage to leap through in its attempt to avoid vaccination but it was beaten back. Melinda anxiously wanted to know if the cow had been hurt but Emily, capturing the spirit of the moment, shouted 'Beat cow!' and pranced around brandishing a stick.

Having proved we were capable of bush camping, Hugh and Mmatsela suggested we all went to Khutse Game Reserve at Easter.

Veronica and Tanasa were with us on this trip and it was a tight squeeze as we all travelled in the Nomad. Crammed in the front were four adults while the children travelled in the back with 80 litres of petrol, 50 litres of water, several bags of food and numerous dolls and blankets.

We drove south to Gaborone then headed northwest to Molepolole, often referred to as the Gateway to the Kalahari. From there the road became more like a sandy track which we drove along for 180 km until we reached the entrance to the game reserve. We had to sign in at the rudimentary gate which was manned by Bushman game scouts who lived with their families in a small community by the gate.

Every few kilometres there was a camping sign attached to a pole but, apart from the occasional tent, there was nothing to suggest that the area was a camp site. We slowed down and waved as we passed two ex-pat male teachers from Mochudi drinking outside their tent which was surrounded by cans!

We pulled off the road at a sign that said 'Camping' and parked by a large camel thorn tree giving welcome shade, then set about erecting the tent and collecting firewood. The children were pleased to be out of the car and ran off in different directions looking for wood. Hugh said that it was essential to have a fire burning all night to keep the lions away. I suddenly panicked as I realised that lions are capable of hunting at any time and, thinking that Emily would be small prey, suggested this wasn't a good idea.

'I guess you are right,' said Hugh as he and Adrian dashed after the girls in the long grass. It was probably only a few minutes but my heart didn't stop thumping till they were safely back, proudly carrying a few sticks.

Most of the cooking was done on a camping stove but, as well as frightening lions and keeping us warm, the fire was also good for cooking jacket potatoes.

As before, Melinda, Emily and I slept in the tent. Veronica and Tanasa slept in the car with Adrian on the roof while Mmatsela and Hugh were on the ground between the tent and the car. I woke briefly in the night to the distant cry of jackals but, relieved it wasn't the roar of a lion, I went back to sleep.

It was Easter Sunday and after a good breakfast we set off for Moreswe Pan about fifty kilometres into Khutse game reserve. The name Khutse means 'where one kneels to drink' in Sekwena which is the local dialect of Tswana. In the distant past the area was once home to Africa's largest inland lake and a series of salt pans are a legacy from that time.

I drove while Adrian and Hugh sat on the roof looking out for game. Occasionally they had to duck to avoid low hanging branches.

I slowed down when we saw a herd of hartebeest in the distance. They were smaller than the kudu we had seen on the way to the cattle post and their curved horns were smaller but they were still impressive. Later we got a better view as more hartebeest ran across the road in front of us, moving gracefully almost as if they were hurdling.

We took it in turns to sit on the roof. I was taking my turn with Hugh and Veronica when Hugh suddenly shouted 'Lions!' and pushed me though the car window which we quickly closed. A lion and lioness were sleeping under a tree but when we reversed the car to get a better view they ambled away.

As we neared the pan we saw ostriches and a secretary bird which was flying very low. We stopped to watch as it landed and strutted along pecking at the ground. Early settlers had named it because of its quill-like black-tipped feathers which give the appearance of a secretary with quill pens tucked behind the ears. It was a magnificent bird, its orange face contrasted with the white feathers of its body and the sheeny black of its spindly legs.

The midday sun beat down and I felt sweat trickling down my legs. I was beginning to find the vastness of the Kalahari overwhelming when we arrived at the pan. Convinced that the shimmering white calcite was water, the children were amazed when we drove into the middle. At this time of the year this should not have been possible but, due to the lack of rain, the pan was dry.

We had been up early and it was time to head back to the campsite. After a picnic lunch we took the route leading to the Central Kalahari game reserve in the hope of seeing giraffe. When we reached what we presumed was the border the track became overgrown. Adrian and Hugh got out and were very excited when they detected lion spoor. I was driving at the time and, seeing that Mmatsela was more terrified than me at the prospect of coming close to lions, I said I would drive five km instead of the ten they suggested. In the event, I drove painstakingly slowly and turned round after three km.

On the way back we stopped and tied a dead tree behind the car so that we would have enough firewood to see us through the night. The evening passed pleasantly under the clear starlit night. In the distance we could see lightning and heard the distant roll of thunder so we went to bed early. The talk of lions must have excited Emily and when Mmatsela was in her sleeping bag she crawled out of the tent and growled at her then toddled back to the tent chuckling!

The storm hit us soon after midnight. Mmatsela came into our tiny tent while Adrian and Hugh bundled our scattered possessions undercover then Hugh joined Tanasa and Veronica in the Nomad. Adrian put his sleeping bag into a large plastic bag, put a hat on his head and slept till morning.

We were up at six.am on Easter Monday, a bit chilly but excited to see hartebeest bounding past our camp. Two seemed particularly interested in what we were doing and stood looking at us for quite a while.

After breakfast we packed up camp and drove slowly towards the gate. We had just arrived at the last pan when a large herd of gemsbok crossed in front of us. Melinda was shouting with excitement as she tried to count them but there must have been over a hundred of them. Gemsbok, known as oryx in some parts of the world, sometimes lose an antler which originally gave rise to tales of the mythical unicorn.

'I wonder if we'll see any more animals,' I said after we left the game reserve.

'We must keep our eyes peeled,' Adrian replied as he drove slowly along the bush road.

'Well, we've certainly seen a lot; even lions!' I shivered slightly.

'Puff adder!' shouted Hugh suddenly and Adrian slammed on the brakes.

'No Hugh!' cried Mmatsela as he and Adrian jumped out of the car for a closer look.

'I can't see a snake,' I said as I leant out of the window.

'That's because it's well camouflaged so it won't be recognised and can wait for its prey.'

'Hey!' shouted Mmatsela as the men tapped it with a stick. At this it puffed itself up and hissed loudly.

There were gasps from the girls and excited chatter as we watched the puff adder slither slowly across the road. It was a non-descript grey and we could just about make out the darker markings on its back.

'Snake gone,' said Emily when it disappeared into the undergrowth at the side of the road.

'Weren't we lucky!' Adrian beamed as he and Hugh got back into the car.

'Very,' said Hugh. 'Puff adders can lie still for several weeks waiting for prey to pass.'

'I'm glad it wasn't you,' I murmured.

'They only bite people if you stand on them.' Hugh turned to the children, 'So you must look carefully where you walk.'

My throat felt dry after all the excitement and I passed round the water.

The girls were beginning to get fidgety when Adrian said 'Tortoise ahead', and stopped the car as it ambled slowly in front of us.

Later on we saw baboons and quickly closed the windows as we knew they liked to jump on cars in search of food.

We were all pleased to get back on to a tarred road at Molepolole. As we began to meet more traffic we saw an injured dog, limping pitifully.

'Look Mummy!' said Melinda, 'there's a dog leaning to hop!'

It was late afternoon when we arrived in Mochudi and the neighbours' children were waiting to hear about our adventure. Tanasa was quite a star as she described all the animals we had seen especially the lions. Her account was accompanied by gasps from the children as they held their hands to their mouths in amazement.

It was good to be clean again and sleep in a bed but I relived the trip when, the following day, I wrote a long letter to my parents describing the memorable weekend.

Chapter 7

Crèche, Winter and a Birthday

Melinda and Tanasa had enjoyed being together on our trip but sadly Tanasa left Mochudi to return to her mother soon afterwards.

However, Melinda was as pleased to see her friend Tina at crèche as I was to see Nora so it was a disappointment when Nora told me they were going on three months leave.

A new family from England moved to the secondary school with two little girls. Sue was a primary school teacher and she not only brought her children to crèche but organised activities that were both educational and enjoyable.

My application for funding for the Day Care Centre was in the process of being approved by USAID and I now had the title of Project Supervisor. One morning I received a message saying that some of the YMCA committee members were needed at the US embassy at two o'clock that afternoon. They were happy to leave their jobs for an essential trip to Gaborone. It was fortunate we arrived at the embassy early because we found that we had been given the wrong message and the embassy people wanted to meet us at the Day Care Centre at two o'clock! However, our early arrival gave us time to go over the application forms and we arranged to meet back in Mochudi later in the afternoon.

The next problem was that as soon as the committee ladies saw the shops they disappeared! Fortunately I found them in the shopping mall and, after driving at break-neck speed, we were only a few minutes late. The Embassy officials were chatting to Beatrice and a rather anxious Miss Kgobe when we arrived.

It had been worth the effort because the outcome was we would soon be able to spend 3,000 pula on equipment and improvements to the facilities.

The nights became colder as winter approached. I raised my eyebrows when Hugh suggested we all went into the bush to collect firewood.

'It's quite safe, there are no lions here,' he laughed.

We drove a short distance out of town and soon had enough kindling and wood to cut into logs to keep us warm in the evenings.

When we first arrived in Mochudi I had been surprised to see a fireplace in the main room of our house but was grateful for it in the short winter season. In the mornings I often saw people swaddled in blankets as they walked to work. I was particularly intrigued by a teacher who wore a long fur coat; I could understand this in the morning but not in the afternoon when the temperature climbed to around 14°C.

The children, however, continued to play barefoot outside and refused to wear even a cardigan. At crèche we were able to keep the children inside for longer with the new toys and equipment we had bought. We tried to insist they wore shoes outside but that was a losing battle.

In the meantime Adrian was busy travelling to schools over a wide area and also preparing for a big trip to remote schools in the Kalahari.

Both the girls had snuffles and a couple of days after Adrian left for his two week trip Emily seemed to be running a temperature.

I decided not to go to crèche and felt bad that there was no way of getting in touch to let them know.

The girls were playing quietly with their dolls when Mmatsela called.

'I saw the car outside and wondered if you were all right.'

'Sela!' said Emily happily and began to run towards her but suddenly sat on the floor in a violent fit of coughing.

'She's worse this morning,' I said anxiously as I knelt beside her.

'You should take her to the hospital.'

'I suppose so.' If I had been in England I would have bought some cough mixture but the nearest pharmacy was in Gaborone.

'Dr Moffat is a very good doctor'.

'Yes, I've heard we are lucky to have him in charge of the hospital. It's just,' I paused, 'I didn't expect it to be so cold!'

Mmatsela nodded. 'It is too cold here, the north of Botswana is warmer.'

'In England it's usually colder in the north!' I gave myself a mental shake. 'Anyway, you are right, Emily needs to see a doctor.'

'I'll call again this afternoon to see how she is.'

'Thanks.' As Mmatsela left I knew I was lucky to have a good friend nearby especially when Adrian was away.

Half an hour later I drove through town, past the Kgotla and up the hill towards the hospital. A woman with a baby on her back and an elderly man were trudging towards the hospital entrance. I couldn't see anywhere to park so I turned into a lane and stopped by what I guessed were the staff houses. They had attractive front gardens and views across the town.

'I hope it's all right to park here,' I said as a woman about my age came out of one of the houses.

'It's fine, have you come to see my husband?'

'Dr Moffat? Yes, my daughter has a cough. And my husband is away', I added rather unnecessarily.

She smiled sympathetically. 'I hope you won't have to wait too long but it's good you've missed the early morning rush.'

I lifted Emily out of the car.

'My sister is going to see the doctor,' announced Melinda tugging at my arm.

'You have a lovely garden,' I said as we turned to go.

'We are lucky. But I don't know how long we'll be staying.'

In fact they moved when Dr Moffat was transferred to run the large hospital in Gaborone and we didn't meet again.

I found out that he was descended from the Scottish missionary Dr Moffat who worked in South Africa and was David Livingstone's father-in-law. Years later I came across him in the fictional Number One Lady Detective books by Alexander McCall Smith.

Bertha was hanging out the washing when we arrived back. 'Dumela Mma, how is the little one?' she asked looking at Emily with concern.

I explained that she had a chest infection and the doctor had given her some antibiotics.

'He said that she must keep warm and wear extra clothes when she plays outside. He was very kind'.

Bertha nodded. 'He is a good doctor. I have prepared some soup, I think Emily will like it.'

Soon after we had eaten, Mmatsela came to see how Emily was.

'Medicine nasty,' said Emily screwing up her face.

'It's Emily's birthday next week and we are going to have a party,' announced Melinda.

'That's exciting, how old will you be?'

'Four!'

'No Emily, you will be two,' I said firmly.

'Will Adrian be here in time for the party?' asked Mmatsela.

'No, but we can have another celebration when he is.'

'I hope he is having a good trip, the Kalahari is cold at this time of year.'

'He didn't know where he would be staying but I suppose there will be places.'

'Maybe.' Mmatsela looked sceptical then pointed to Emily curled up on the settee. 'I think she needs to go to bed. Shall I take Melinda? We can do some baking.'

'Thank you. You'd like to go with Mmatsela, wouldn't you?'

'Yes!' Melinda picked up her doll and ran to the door.

'Send her back if she's any trouble,' I said and silently added 'But not too soon.'

The next day I left Emily with Bertha and dropped Melinda at crèche. Sue offered to bring her home and, by the end of the morning Emily was feeling a lot better. However I kept her away from the other children when they called after school to hang around on Melinda's climbing bar.

The cold weather continued and we huddled in bed to open Emily's presents and cards from us and from Adrian's parents.

She was excited about going to crèche in the morning and, as was the custom, everyone sang Happy Birthday and clapped.

On our way back we stopped at the Education Office to check our post. In her last letter, my mother said she had posted Emily's present but unfortunately it hadn't arrived. However, there was a parcel from her sister, Dorothy, or Auntie Doff as we called her.

'There's a present for me too!' said Melinda as she helped Emily rip open the parcel as soon as we got home.

I was nearly as excited as them because, inside the parcel, were two glove puppets. They were a touching reminder of my childhood, for it was Auntie Doff's husband who had made my first puppet theatre.

I showed the girls how to use them and Emily delighted in creeping up and poking, first me and then a very surprised Bertha, with a puppet and speaking in a squeaky voice.

'You must take care of them, puppets don't like to go outside,' I said as I realised they wouldn't last long if they were dropped in the sand.

I was glad they had the puppets to keep them amused till Sue and her children came in the afternoon with handmade cards and a book.

Emily proudly showed them the puppets and I sensed we could have a problem with sharing. However, Sue soon showed us how to make puppets for everyone by drawing a face on her forefinger which she then waggled through a hole in a piece of tissue. This kept them all amused until it was time for birthday cake.

'That's a big cake,' remarked Sue as we tucked in.

'I made a big one so that we can share it with the children across the road when they return from school.'

'Oh! That's nice of you.' Sue sounded surprised.

They left soon afterwards but the party continued outside as Mmatsela and Veronica arrived and we were joined by the other children.

Melinda was sad that Adrian wasn't there for Emily's birthday but I promised he would be home soon and we would have another party then.

Chapter 8

Kalahari Workshops

Letter from Adrian to our Parents

The course of my work takes me to schools the length and breadth of Botswana. On this occasion I travelled with Ted and also Martha Greenhow, a Mennonite teacher from Canada.

The Land Rover was put in for a thorough overhaul. We put a 200 litre drum of petrol on board, together with several jerry cans of petrol, camp beds, water, food, cooking equipment and teaching aids. Ted and I made an early start in order to meet Martha before dark.

The first 100 km was on a good tarred road. However, the road across the Kalahari to Ghanzi via Jwaneng was very rough because all the soft sand had been graded off which jarred the suspension and our bodies. Jwaneng used to be a small cattle post where one or two herders and their families lived. Then along came De Beers, found diamonds and, whoosh, now there is a very busy township growing up.

We passed the turn-off for Jwaneng and headed for the Kalahari Desert. Desert is a misleading name for this sea of dried grass and shrub savanna. It's a desert only because there is no surface water. Below the sands there is usually water although people may have to drill three hundred metres to find it.

We stopped for lunch on a windswept plain, mile upon mile of dry grass to the east of the road and miles of burnt grass to the west. We sat in the sun to keep warm and let the silence of the place refresh our tired bodies.

The road after that went on for miles, absolutely straight. The driving wasn't easy as the majority of vehicles using the road are lorries with a much wider wheel track and had consequently carved out two great furrows that our wheels didn't fit into.

We saw ostrich but no other wild animals though there were plenty of cattle within reach of boreholes. As one approaches a borehole the grass disappears and thorn scrub invades the area. The road next to the borehole is well churned sand and as slippery as fine snow or ice. At one place we had to use not only four wheel drive but also the low gear ratio.

Just as it was getting dark we arrived at Kaang to meet Martha who had travelled up from Tsabong near the South African border. We were going to stay at a medical outreach post. The nurses' house was empty and, for a moment, we wondered if we were going to have to camp but then the Swiss nursing sisters and their other guests arrived from their evening stroll. Conversation was stilted as we were tired, having driven something like 600 km in ten hours. During the night there were many comings and goings as the nurses delivered another child into this wold.

Morning seemed to come round faster each day of the trip. We set off for Ghanzi but branched off the 'main road' to visit a school set up by the German Volunteer Service that taught the Basarawa (Bushman) children. The children surrounded our Land Rover and I heard one of the Basarawa languages for the first time. It was full of various clicks and where these languages have been written down they are designated by the symbols !, *, /, &, // which makes it an impossible language to learn other than in the field. The school has its own borehole, the only visible sign being a diesel engine driving a pump which was filling a large concrete reservoir. There is another borehole nearby at Lone Tree which occasionally breaks down; when it does the thousands of cattle that depend on it become rather troublesome to the school. Even though the compound is fenced, the cattle smash their way through the gate and even bite taps off to get at the water. It is reported that they can find buried water pipes, dig them up and break them open with their hooves. Needless to say, class is dismissed at the *first sign of invasion and the intruders beaten ruthlessly till they leave.*

After we had coffee we set off for Ghanzi. The road became much worse and it was obvious which parts were really bad by the large number of branches in the road, put there by drivers of two wheel drive vehicles to make a mat that was drivable on. We heard the story of one person who became stuck, dug out and stuck again for twenty hours in one three kilometre stretch.

Finally we drove into a village and had views of something different to acacia scrub. After driving 280 km we saw a beautiful sunset over a vast plain of golden grass just before we arrived in Ghanzi. It was 7 o'clock and Ted and I decided to stay at the Kalahari Arms Hotel which is amazingly like a real hotel. Martha and her driver pressed on to Xanagas as she was expected there and people get worried if one doesn't arrive. (They did eventually arrive at 1030 pm.) Ted and I had a large T-bone steak each followed by long baths and what seemed like another very short night's sleep.

Over breakfast we were regaled with the manager's snake stories. They were troubled by a family of Egyptian cobras living and breeding under the paving slabs leading to the car park. The manager had the bright idea of pouring petrol down all the cracks and, after pouring a trail away from the path, lit the safe end. The flames rushed along the trail and seemed to go out as it got to the path. Just before he went to investigate the whole path blew up, concrete flying everywhere. And the snakes haven't been seen since!

The second story concerned a boomslang, highly venomous, that was spied in the branches of a tree in the compound. A man was called to bring his rifle and shoot it out of the tree. Instead of shooting its head he shot it clean in half. The front half jumped out of the tree and chased the onlookers till it was dispatched by a second shot. As everyone was recovering from this a rather crotchety customer was going on about their collective cowardice when the back half fell on his head. He joined the ranks of the cowards.

On this note we left the hotel, filled up with petrol and headed for Xanagas. The first 5 km out of Ghanzi were totally overgrazed. All that was growing were dull green bushes. After this we drove through farms that displayed great variance in management, from almost bare to knee high grass. The farms are here because the water is near enough the surface to be pumped by wind pumps. The majority are owned by Boers who were allowed to settle here by the Botswana government in the last century to stop German encroachment from their colony South West Africa (Namibia).

When we arrived at Xanagas Martha was in full swing giving a demonstration lesson, so Ted and I started work as well. The school is a boarding school with quite a number of Basarawa children. The children were very receptive and their English was good, as it was in all the schools in this district. In the afternoon we had a short workshop where the teachers made a few aids then we transferred our belongings to Martha's Chev (Chevrolet) truck and set off for Makunda.

We arrived after dark, made up our beds in various classrooms and I cooked a scrumptious meal after which we soon retired for the night.

After breakfast I took the truck back to a farm we had seen on our way in. I hoped someone had the necessary equipment to solder the radiator up as it had sprung a leak and, as the nearest garage was at Ghanzi, I thought a farm was likely to help. Thankfully, the first place I tried had a blow torch so all was fixed in about an hour and they were almost offended when I asked how much.

I was back at the school in time to give a demonstration lesson on pin-hole cameras which I got the children to make themselves. After this, a bit of science, I got them to tell me how they had made them. We had a short workshop then drove to Kule.

It was only 120 km but it took three hours of hard driving. As we were driving along we saw some hartebeest and lots of spoor in the road. We expected at any moment to come across a vast herd of them. We turned a corner and there across the horizon was a vast herd of cows. Oh well, you can't have it all ways!

A bit further on we had to get off the track to let a lorry go the way we had come. Had it been flying the Jolly Roger, no one would have been surprised. However, the stubbly unwashed Boar farmer came over and apologised. 'Couldn't get off the road,' he said, 'both front brakes and shock absorbers are broken.'

We were having difficulty staying on the road with a full complement of springs and were amazed how far he had travelled with broken brakes and shock absorbers.

'Is there any game up ahead?'

'Yes, and we've got a shooting licence but have run out of bullets!'

As we had enquired in order to look at and photograph the game, we were slightly taken aback by the doleful reply.

We stayed the night in an empty teacher's house and went on to Ncojane, near the Namibian boarder, the following morning. There was a great heap of mud just inside the school gates which, on enquiry, we found had been a classroom. A couple of months after the council opened a new classroom it fell down!

We left there about 3.30 pm and drove back to Kule for the night, doing the 25 km in an hour. As we pulled up there was the sound of singing and dancing coming from a classroom. The Basarawa children were practising for a national competition. They were dressed in traditional costumes but wouldn't dance outside as they didn't want their parents to criticize too much. Just once in the evening, the rhythm, mood, and atmosphere combined for about three minutes and produced an excellent piece of dancing. The rest of the time it was very good but I felt there was no magic to it.

After the children's performance it was very odd the next morning to see them dressed in their school uniforms.

Why pin hole cameras? I feel a great need to justify what I am doing. The children are so much part of the twentieth century, they rely on diesel pumps to pump water from boreholes drilled by other engines. The stars in the sky have their serenity interrupted by satellites. The children can tell the distance between a D.C.10 and a 747 at eleven thousand metres. So I suppose I don't have to justify my work too much.

We had a teacher's workshop in the afternoon and were rather surprised at the time it took one of the teachers to make a four piece jigsaw.

We packed up and drove back to Xanagas for the weekend. We drove along the South West Africa/Namibia border where both countries have erected a fence to keep each other's cattle from being infected with foot and mouth disease. We saw a female kudu and her young, ostriches and a magnificent male kudu; the job certainly has nice perks!

We hit the main road at Mamuno and slaked our thirst with a cold sprite at its bottle store. The border football teams were practising for a match with Nocojane United, at least four hours hard driving away, and are their nearest rivals.

When we arrived at Xanagas, rather than disrupt a classroom, I decided to put my camp bed outside between the Martins' rondavals. I was rewarded with a wonderful sky and an almost full moon to act as a night light and, as I was in a sleeping bag inside another sleeping bag I wasn't affected by the near freezing temperatures. Though I woke up rather startled to find a cat sleeping on my head, the cat was also startled when it found itself flying through the air. At dawn it was the turn of the labrador to inflict itself on me with similar results though it didn't fly as far as the cat.

Saturday was a super day. After breakfast Dale and Lori Martin, Mennonite volunteers, took us to the place where they are drilling for water. This is to provide water for cattle in a Basarawa settlement they are setting up. This was the *third hole they were drilling and it seemed it was to be successful because, just the day before, the drillers struck water at 140 me. Dale and Lori were trying not to be excited about it because they had been drilling for two years and this was the third site. The water was slightly saline but apparently that is beneficial for the cattle, it didn't taste too bad either. At Xanagas the cattle drink waste water and seem to thrive on it, I would need to be quite thirsty before I could succumb to that though. The drillers were Batswana but their 'roustabouts' were Basarawa, so I had a chance to have a good look at their more permanent dwellings. They are dome shaped, made of branches stuck into the ground at one end, the tops are then tied together with bark 'string' and the whole rudimentary thatched. There is an opening to allow access that is about a third of the total diameter and in the middle of this there was evidence of nightly fires. The rest of the area resembled a western style camp site with a camp fire and cooking area and lines between trees to air bedding made from animal skin blankets. Some children were playing on a swing made of a leather rope tied to a branch put there especially for them.*

On our way from Kalkfontein to the Martins we stopped at a tower built on the South West African border at latitude 22° south and longitude 21° east. On a map the border is shown as a right angle at this point. It is a legacy of the colonial division of Africa with little regard to local settlement patterns.

In all directions, as far as the eye could see, the flat landscape was covered with grass and scrub and, apart from the border fence and narrow dirt road, no sign of human life at all.

When we were back at the Martins' rondaval the sun was high and the buildings warming up. Dale had painted them gloss white to reflect the sun more, this measure lowered the midday summer temperature by 15 C° to a 'cool' 38°C inside the room.

Sunday we lounged about and got both vehicles ready to go on to the next two village schools then on to Ghanzi. We arrived back in Ghanzi a day earlier than we were expected and had a bit of difficulty booking into the hotel as three people were expected the next day. It took ten minutes to persuade them that the three people, Rosser, Hutton and Greenhow, were us and it wasn't just co-incidence that we had the same names!

We had to cut our workshop short on Wednesday afternoon as a magician was in town and giving a show that was not to be missed. However, I did give it a miss as I couldn't face sitting with hundreds of others while being in such areas of vastness.

Thursday we started on our way home, spending the night with Miss Ventera, a missionary running a border primary school. The dorms were not ready so we had to sleep in the classrooms because the children destined for the dorms slept in Miss Ventera's house, 56 girls in a two bedroom house! The standard two children were, in some ways as capable as the standard five children in other schools. I discovered that the store rooms in these schools could be converted into a camera obscura.

From here, Kuki, we drove north to Maun via Lake Ngami. This shallow lake used to be flanked with every kind of game. Now there are an estimated one million cattle on its shores – progress!

In Maun we stayed at the Island Safari Hotel on the banks of Thamalakani River, the sight of so much water was soothing. After another night's sleep that seemed to last five minutes we set off for Mochudi at 7.30 am. 900 km later we arrived, having stopped only once, to refuel.

It was 8 pm when I managed to look at my watch through Melinda's cuddles.

Chapter 9

A Royal Visit and Non-Formal Education

The week after Adrian returned from his Kalahari trip he went to Gaborone to report back to Bram, his boss. While he was there he met Wolfgang, a German science teacher based in Ramotswa on the South African border.

He said he would like to see some of the schools in Mochudi so Adrian invited him to stay a couple of nights. Wolfgang told us that he didn't like living so close to South Africa and had asked Bram for a transfer to Maun in the north west of Botswana.

'I stayed there the last night of my Kalahari trip,' said Adrian.

'We plan to take my parents there when they come at Christmas,' I added.'

'I want to go canoeing in the Okavango Delta. It's the best way to see the wildlife especially the hippos in the river.'

'That might be a bit too close for my Mum and Dad.'

I was unable to share Wolfgang's enthusiasm for danger but said that we would love to visit him if he was transferred to Maun.

'Are you going to see your Queen tomorrow?' asked Beatrice excitedly when we arrived at crèche on July 26th.

'I don't think I'm invited,' I laughed.

'People will be cheering her in Gaborone.'

I knew that Queen Elizabeth was visiting Botswana on her way to attend the Commonwealth Conference in Zambia but the Government had not declared a public holiday.

'You must tell us all about it.' Beatrice seemed certain that we would be there.

Hugh called early next morning to suggest we went to see the royal visitors, so we all piled into the Nomad and drove to Gaborone.

It was a cool morning and we found a place in the sun outside Botsalano House where the Queen was viewing the Orapa diamonds.

We happened to be standing near his boss so Adrian asked him if he could have the morning off for the royal visit. Bram nodded his assent with a smile and pointed to all the ministry people who should have been at their desks. It was interesting seeing so many of them close up including the Chief of Police, an Englishman who had taken Botswana citizenship.

The cheering began as soon as the royal party was spotted and we were caught up in the excitement of seeing the Queen who was wearing an attractive emerald green outfit. She seemed particularly petite as she walked next to Botswana's President, Seretse Khama, while Prince Philip and Lady Khama were several paces behind.

We were cordoned off but the Queen shook hands with and spoke to quite a few members of the public. After the procession passed us we ran down some side streets to see Her Majesty further along. Melinda, standing on Adrian's shoulders, had an excellent view but Emily and I were unable to see over people's heads, although it didn't stop Emily from shouting and pointing excitedly.

'Let's go to the Trade Fair,' suggested Hugh after we had caught a glimpse of the royal entourage driving towards the airport.

The Queen had opened the Trade Fair the day before and we were surprised by the lack of crowds. Even more surprising was seeing a small display of the Crown Jewels which particularly impressed Mmatsela and Veronica. Mmatsela was also impressed with the cattle which were bigger than those at her cattle post. Emily, on the other hand, wanted to see the pigs and danced around snorting for several days afterwards.

It was still warm enough to gather on our veranda when we got back. Talk drifted to the problems Seretse and Ruth had from Seretse's tribe and the British government when they married secretly in London in 1948. Seretse's father was Kgosi, Chief, of the Bamangwato whose capital was Serowe in Central Botswana. He died in 1925 when Seretse was four years old and his uncle was appointed guardian and regent until Seretse was able to take up his duties as Kgosi. After attending college in South Africa, Seretse studied at Balliol College, Oxford.

When we told people of my parents' generation that we were going to Botswana they generally asked what the country used to be called. Many of them had heard of Bechuanaland and would speak fondly of 'Our Ruth' who, despite opposition from the British government, had married an African king. They had met when Seretse was studying to be a barrister in London and Ruth was working for Lloyds of London.

'I never really understood the British government's opposition to the marriage,' I said as we watched our daughters playing with their Batswana friends.'

'They didn't want to ruffle South African feathers,' replied Hugh. 'South Africa was terrified of independent black-controlled territories on its borders in case their own majority black population seized power.'

'But we've always opposed apartheid!'

Hugh shook his head. 'Theoretically we do now but Britain still relies on South Africa for minerals especially gold and diamonds.'

'But Botswana has diamonds.'

'We had a narrow escape; diamonds weren't discovered here until after Independence. It might have been a different story if it had happened before.'

'And we were lucky to have a good man to be our first Prime Minister, and now our President,' added Mmatsela.

We were interrupted by shrieks as Melinda and the bigger girls started running round the house followed by Emily and Tumo struggling to keep up.

'I think it's time for the kids to cool down,' I said as I got up to get some drinks.

Beatrice and Miss Kgobe wanted to know all about the Royal visit when we arrived at crèche the next day and were a little bemused when all Emily wanted to talk about was the pigs. However I was able to give a more detailed account of the day which had been a welcome change from our daily routine. I was beginning to feel the pressure of making sure that the Day Care Centre met all the requirements of the American donors, including enlisting and overseeing the work of local builders to improve the facilities.

A few days later, Adrian came back from the Education Office with the news that another English couple had arrived and were living near the kgotla.

George and Heather had been sent by IVS, International Voluntary Service, to work in the newly formed Department of Non-Formal Education which had been set up to provide basic literacy programmes and also enable people to continue their education informally.

When we visited them we found their accommodation was also 'non-formal'.

We parked near the kgotla and asked an elderly man if he knew where the new English couple lived.

We were slightly surprised when he pointed to two rondavals in a small courtyard.

When we got nearer we saw two ex-pats sitting near the entrance. They waved and stood up as we introduced ourselves.

'I'm George,' said a friendly red-haired man.

'And I'm Heather, another Heather!' his wife said in a softly spoken voice.

'Welcome to Mochudi', Adrian held out his hand. 'How are you settling in?'

'It's certainly interesting being in the centre of things here.'

I looked around, and smiled at a Motswana woman sitting outside one of the huts who waved at us.

'Is this your house?' asked Melinda in amazement as she and Emily poked their heads into the rondaval.

'Yes, would you like to see inside?' Heather said tentatively.

The first thing I noticed was what looked like a door balancing on top of some breeze blocks. On top was a typewriter and piles of papers.

'Welcome to our office,' said George with a mock flourish.

'Do you sleep in the other rondaval?' I asked.

'No that's Theresa's house. We just have this one room.'

At that point Melinda whispered in my ear.

'Do you have a toilet?' I asked Heather.

She shook her head. 'We share a pit latrine with next door. Come I'll take you,' she said holding out her hand to Melinda.

She was happy to go with Heather while Emily explored the compound.

George explained they were waiting for a room to become available for their office and a government house for them to live in.

'In the meantime, it's interesting here and we get to see what's going on at the kgotla. The day after we arrived there was a procession of several hundred young men going into the bush for their initiation ceremony. It's the first time it's been done for years and apparently it's quite a spectacle when they come back in couple of weeks.'

'You've got ringside seats.' Adrian was impressed.

'I'm thirsty,' Melinda announced when she came back from the latrine.

Guessing that George and Heather weren't geared up for providing children's drinks, I said that it was time to go home and suggested that they came for lunch the following Saturday.

As always the girls were excited about having visitors and were busy drawing pictures to give them which were graciously received.

Over lunch we exchanged experiences and were interested that, like us, this wasn't their first overseas posting. They had been in Botswana two years earlier and after a spell working in England they decided to return.

We were pleased to hear that premises had been found for their office near the kgotla.

'That will give you more space although it will be better for you when you move up here and have your own kitchen and bathroom,' I said.

'Have the young men returned from the initiation?' asked Adrian.

'Yes, it was quite a spectacle with lots of drumming and a big welcome by Chief Linchwe. Apparently it was his idea to revive the practice.'

'It's good to see some traditional customs returning. We were beginning to think there weren't any.'

'Oh there definitely are,' laughed George. 'There was an accusation of witchcraft only this week. Theresa found a dead bat outside her door and accused our neighbour of putting it there deliberately.'

'The nice neighbour with the toilet?' I asked.

'Yes, there was quite a kerfuffle. Obviously she hadn't put it there but they aren't speaking now.'

'Maybe it was toilet envy', I murmured.

'It was probably motivated by jealousy. Anyway we managed to keep out of it and are still speaking to them both.'

After lunch the girls ran outside to play with the neighbours' children while we told them about Adrian's Kalahari workshops and our forthcoming trip round Botswana. I explained that Adrian's boss had given permission for us all to go and I was really looking forward to it.

Chapter10

Bush Fire and Bush Mechanics

Ted was still on leave and Eleanor, who was based in Selebi-Phikwe, a copper-nickel mining town in the Central District, was looking forward to joining Adrian and Martha on the Kalahari workshop trip. However, she was not pleased when she found out that Bram had given permission for Melinda and Emily to come too, especially as she had hoped to take her dog.

Eleanor stayed with us overnight and we left early the next morning, our Land Rover packed high with camping equipment and food for two weeks plus a mass of teaching aids, films, a projector, a generator and 200 litres of petrol. We were to spend our first week with Martha in Tsabong in the far South East of Botswana.

The morning was cool and the girls were still sleepy so they snuggled into sleeping bags laid across camping mattresses on top of the luggage. They were fine for the first 140 km then they needed me to hold on to them as the truck lurched through the sand. Adrian and Eleanor shared the driving. The next 11 hours was like driving for hundreds of miles along the furrows of a ploughed field which happened to be one of 'main roads' across Botswana.

Melinda and Emily were constantly on the lookout for animals but all we saw on this part of the trip was a bush cat. The stars were bright and it was very cold when we pulled up at Tsabong police station at 9 o'clock to ask the way to Martha's house.

Martha welcomed us warmly and, despite organising food and accommodation for 50 teachers as well as running workshops, she ensured that we were comfortable.

Left to our own devices, the next morning the girls and I set off to explore. Tsabong is the only part of the Kalahari Desert that actually looks like desert, complete with sand dunes. We wrapped up warmly to protect ourselves from the chilly wind and headed for the dune at the end of Martha's road. It was heavy going as we kept sinking into the sand but the prospect of rolling down the dune made the children rush up tirelessly then, shrieking with delight, they would roll down again. After a while we decided to make for the very top. Somebody had built a thatched house at the summit and I wondered if he had chosen it for the view it commanded of the village with a rocky dune to the west and the unending expanse of desert in all directions. We looked down at two men on horse-back at the foot of the dune and a sledge loaded with firewood pulled by donkeys.

The following day we were surprised to find how much our legs ached as a result of walking through the deep sand so we decided to explore the flat areas of the village. The two general stores were well stocked with basic essentials and we were able to buy a cold drink. We passed the bore hole which supplies the village with water; the nearest river only runs two or three times a century.

Then we visited the kraal where the police camels were kept. Camels are easier than horses for trekking in the sand and they are bred specially, one was only three weeks old. Training does not begin until camels are eight years old and the process takes a few years. The highlight of the week was our ride on a camel, Melinda and Emily waved gaily from what seemed a very long way up. We paraded past the police fuel depot and I smiled at the incongruous picture of a camel standing next to a petrol pump.

I cooked for the six of us in the evenings then Adrian, Martha and Eleanor put on film shows for the teachers. A favourite was Creatures of the Namib Desert, made by the National Geographic Society. All the village came to watch. There were fearful gasps as a sidewinder snake sidled across the screen and, closely behind, a prehistoric looking chameleon with jaws wide open. However, this changed to laughter when a back flip spider scuttled into view, followed by a large female intent on finding a mate.

We had planned to make an early start for the long drive to Ghanzi, with an overnight stop at a game reserve along the way. However, there was so much to sort out at the end of the course that it was mid-afternoon by the time we left. Martha gave lifts to several teachers and they proved an invaluable help when her Chevrolet truck broke down. The first time this happened was only five minutes after starting the journey, followed by another three before Adrian finally managed to fix the petrol switch.

The stops enabled the girls and I to look at the spring flowers. There were white daisies, different varieties of pink and purple flowers and thorn trees covered with fragrant white blossom.

A faulty petrol switch was not a problem Martha had been expecting. She had been more worried that her truck would have problems getting stuck in the sand as her four wheel drive had broken. It was becoming dark the first time the Chev got stuck and we decided to continue at first light. We pitched our little tent between the two vehicles in the middle of the road and Martha's passengers lit a fire. A full moon rose as we shared the food we had brought for our overnight stop and listened to the kek-kek-kek call of barking geckos searching for a mate. Melinda looked worried but Martha explained that they were small lizards who liked to sing at night from their burrows in the sand.

We settled down for the night; Martha and Eleanor in the vehicles, Adrian outside our tent and Martha's passengers around the fire.

I roused everyone at six o'clock and by eight thirty we had managed to dig Martha's truck out and were on our way. After that we lost track of the number of times we had to dig Martha out.

In the afternoon we came to the game reserve where we had hoped to stay the previous night and drove slowly, keeping a look out for wildlife. Suddenly we came upon a large herd of galloping hartebeest, followed by wildebeest running full pelt. A few minutes later we saw a flock of ostriches also running as if away from something.

Soon afterwards I noticed a whiff of smoke and wondered if we were nearing a bushman village. The next streak of smoke was more worrying, this was no small bushman fire. As we drew nearer, the sky became filled with black smoke. Ahead of us was a fire crackling on either side of the track.

We stopped well back to investigate. Flames were leaping and sparks were flying across the track. However Adrian reckoned it would be easy enough to drive through, provided the vehicles didn't get stuck in the sand.

To reduce the risk he and Martha's driver, a young man of about 20 only employed that week, shovelled sand over the burning scrub nearest the track.

Even with the windows closed the acrid smoke infiltrated the vehicle and I felt my throat burning as I held tightly onto the children.

Worried about the amount of fuel on board, they worked fast and it wasn't long before we were able to drive quickly through, leaving the blackened vegetation behind.

It had been a long day and the girls were fast asleep when we finally arrived at the village of Kang in the centre of what was later known as the Trans-Kalahari Highway. Martha knew it would be all right to stay with the two nursing sisters at the small medical outpost there. They were amazed but also delighted when we carried in two sleeping children. They told us the next morning how special it was to see healthy and lively children because a quarter of the children in the village had recently died of measles.

The next 70 km took eight hours as we had to stop regularly to dig out Martha's truck. It wasn't just sand around the wheels that caused a problem, sometimes Adrian had to lie down and get the sand from under the axle.

As far as the children were concerned it was just one glorious sandpit. Melinda climbed onto the Land Rover cab and jumped off accompanied by gleeful shouts from Emily of 'Jump Minna 'gain!'

On several occasions our Land Rover managed to tow the Chev but our rope kept breaking. People along the road who helped us said that once we reached Lone Tree the road got better so we celebrated by finishing the food and hot drinks. By this time we had dropped off all our passengers. Adrian filled the petrol tank from the drums we had on board and estimated that, if we were lucky we would be in Ghanzi by nine o'clock.

Eleanor said she would drive the Land Rover till it got properly dark so Adrian decided to travel with Martha. They set off in front and Eleanor switched on our engine but nothing happened, just that dead engine sound that sends your heart into your boots. I gazed in horror at the sight of the Chev disappearing over the brow of an incline in the middle of the Kalahari at dusk. We knew it could be an hour before they returned because the Chev goes faster and they would probably wait for us to catch up. We flagged down some Boer farmers taking cattle to the abattoir and they did their best to help but it was Adrian who arrived and fixed it half an hour later; the switch between the two petrol tanks wasn't working.

We finally arrived at the hotel in Ghanzi at half past ten to find they hadn't got our booking, the generator wasn't working so there was no electricity and the proprietor had gone to bed with the kitchen keys so we couldn't have a hot drink. We were, however, very grateful to have a bed.

The week in Ghanzi passed pleasantly and uneventfully. There were only 14 teachers on the course so Adrian, Martha and Eleanor had more free time. The South African couple who ran the hotel didn't mind the children in the kitchen or playing with their cats and dogs. I set up school on the hotel veranda much to the interest of the other guests.

There was not much sight-seeing to do as Ghanzi is situated on a plain surrounded by cattle ranches. Unlike many other places, there was a good relationship between the Boer farmers who had moved into the area in the late 1890s and the Bushmen, as well as people from the local Sekgalagadi tribe.

The highlight of the week was watching the plane from Lloyds Bank arrive on its weekly visit. A British agricultural adviser and an officer from the High Commission also flew in from Gaborone for a night. I was embarrassed when I heard Eleanor say to the agriculturist that it was all right for him to fly, whereas we didn't have that luxury. He rebuffed her by saying that when he first did the job he used to travel everywhere on horseback.

At the end of the week we had the choice of returning the way we had come which was more direct or circumnavigating the Kalahari sands by driving north to Maun than east to Francistown where we would be on a tarred road to Gaborone. Although for Martha this was the wrong direction entirely it was for Martha's sake we decided to take this route as she needed to put her truck into a garage in Gaborone.

We planned to spend the first night at Lake Ngami where we hoped to see flamingos. However, things did not go according to plan.

50 km out of Ghanzi we stopped because Adrian was worried about the noises the Land Rover was making. He bent down to look while Martha's driver was digging her truck out for the final time.

'What's up?' asked Eleanor.

'Come and see'.

'I wouldn't be surprised if the engine had fallen out,' Eleanor joked.

'It has!'

For once Adrian wasn't joking. The engine had fallen off its mountings and the gear box wasn't in good shape either.

Once again a helpful farmer stopped and lent us some cable because our tow rope was useless. Martha then towed us back 30 km with the farmer following to make sure we were all right and to show us the workshop run by some Boer farmers. Adrian left us there and continued to the Government workshop in Ghanzi to get some gear box mountings then drove back to the farm where we were waiting. The farmer's wife was friendly and keen to talk about how the life was better than her native South Africa but it wasn't easy living in such an isolated place. She showed me her garden which was beautifully kept, complete with garden gnomes. Melinda and Emily enjoyed playing with her children and the fact that they didn't speak each other's language was no problem.

It was seven o'clock before we continued our journey to stay with a missionary teacher at a small school two hours drive away. When we arrived the house was dark and our hearts sank. However, we knocked and found half a dozen people in a candlelit room sitting at a table laden with good things to eat. We didn't need to say much, they just got extra chairs and handed us platefuls of food.

We then had the energy to bed down in a classroom where Melinda and Emily enjoyed writing on the blackboard before going to bed.

Feeling refreshed we set off early the next day. We were on a narrow bush road with high grass on either side when what appeared to be a white madman hurtled round a bend towards us. I peered forward to scowl at the dangerous driver then shouted, 'Stop! It's Wolfgang!' He was travelling with Mokwathi, a Motswana member of the in-service team who seemed very relieved to stop. They were distributing educational magazines to schools throughout the north west of Botswana and Wolfgang was determined to the do the job quickly. When he told us he had driven for 25 hours, his puppy at his feet, with only brief stops I smiled sympathetically at Mokwathi.

Our next stop was Lake Ngami where we had hoped to camp the previous night. I was interested in going there as it was one of the places David Livingstone had stayed on his trek across the Kalahari after he and his family left Kolobeng. He described it as a shimmering lake, some 130 km long and 30 km wide. Adrian had driven past on his trip in June and been distressed to see dead and dying cattle stuck in the mud as they attempted to reach the lake which had shrunk considerably due to the drought. We looked down from the top of an escarpment and saw it glinting a long way in the distance. After driving slowly down the escarpment we were relieved to see tall grass growing where the mud had been. However, we were unable to see the lake at this level.

'I've heard that it's shrinking more each year,' said Martha.

Now, over 40 years later, Lake Ngami is drying up and animals, including hippos are dying in the mud.

There was no time to look for wildlife after our picnic lunch in a small wooded area and we continued on our way to Maun. The Island Safari Hotel and camp site was out of town, it was eight o'clock on Saturday night and every room had been taken. We weren't too worried as the camp site was nice but, understandably, Eleanor had been looking forward to a room on her own away from two small children.

Sunday passed pleasantly paddling about on a canoe and watching birds and cattle wading into the water. The tall trees and running water were a refreshing change from desert.

As our Land Rover was virtually un-driveable we loaded everything into Martha's truck and left it at the government garage in Maun.

The journey to Francistown was long and dusty but we had a lovely welcome there from Martha's brother who was also working as a volunteer.

Eleanor was most relieved when we dropped her at her house in Selebi-Phikwe on our way back to Mochudi. True to form, we arrived home after dark but were happy that we were finally home in time to celebrate Adrian's 29th birthday.

Chapter 11

Home School, Snakes and Weaver Birds

Our friends were pleased to see us on our return and amazed to hear about all our mishaps.

Beatrice and Miss Kgobe welcomed us as if we had been away from crèche a month rather than two weeks. They were surprised when I told them that in England children started school when they were five and so I would be giving Melinda lessons at home.

'But you will still bring her and Emily to crèche? They will miss their friends.' And we will miss your help; Beatrice's unspoken words hung in the air.

I had enrolled Melinda with WES, the World-wide Education service which supported home schooling for British ex-pats throughout the world. Some of the material had arrived but I was already beginning to wonder how Melinda, with her gregarious nature, would take to one-to-one learning.

'Don't worry, we'll still come to crèche,' I said as I looked across at the girls playing happily.

We had bought Melinda a desk from an auction of government furniture and she was excited that she had her own 'classroom' in the spare bedroom.

A week after our Kalahari trip I explained to Bertha that Melinda would be having 'school' and asked her to keep an eye on Emily for an hour.

Melinda felt quite grown up as she settled down at her desk with a new notebook and pencils.

Unfortunately I hadn't anticipated Emily's desperation to attend school with Melinda. She hammered on the door screaming to come in. I wasn't sure what to do for the best. This first day of school was uncharted territory for both of us and I wanted to get it right. It was a relief for everyone when Mmatsela, who had heard the screams, took Emily to her house.

The following day Emily was happy to help Bertha wash clothes in a tub in the garden while we had a shorter lesson and then went to crèche. After that I decided to let Emily join in the lessons.

WES developed from PNEU, Parents' Educational Union, which was founded in 1887. The methods consisted of three levels. The first level is Atmosphere which means that the child can learn by seeing and doing things that are around them as they grow up. The second is Discipline which means teaching a child how to act and the difference between good and bad. The third level is Life which is about combining what is learned at home, at school and in their surroundings.

Unconsciously we had already exposed Melinda to these methods, particularly on our Kalahari trip. What I hoped from my membership of WES was guidance on how to teach basic skills. However, correspondence was slow and there was little step-by-step guidance on how to teach the fundamentals of reading, writing, arithmetic and spelling.

Drawing and painting was a favourite subject of Melinda's and she often asked Adrian to give her pictures to Bram Swallow. On a visit to Gaborone he was amazed to see the walls of Bram's office covered in Melinda's pictures.

The Botswana Book Centre in Gaborone expanded its children's section and we were regular visitors. I was delighted to find Dick Bruna's delightful Miffy books on sale. On one occasion Emily became so absorbed in looking at one of the books that I couldn't find her and rushed around the shop shouting, 'I've lost my little girl!' She was quickly found but the incident came back to haunt me two years later when I was visiting the shop in my new capacity as a Curriculum Development Officer. The manager greeted me with a sly smile and cried, 'I've lost my little girl!'

It was a lesson for me that, once seen in a certain light it can be difficult to change people's perceptions.

Adrian's work continued to take him to remote schools but he also ran teachers' workshops at the museum where he now had an office. Gill Condy, a botanical illustrator, was also based at the museum. One day she mentioned to Adrian that she was going to look for snakes as she had a commission which included a drawing of a snake. He was, of course, delighted to accompany her.

They walked all over the hill but there were no snakes to be seen. After admiring the view from the top they returned to the museum and Adrian went to pick up his bag from a classroom which was currently used as a store room. He was startled to see a black mamba slithering across the floor and hide behind some boxes. Knowing that it is the second most venomous snake after the king cobra, he edged to the door and called to Sandy Grant, the museum curator. He told Adrian to keep an eye on the snake while he phoned the council. There happened to be a broom against the wall which Adrian grabbed in case he needed a weapon.

He was relieved when two burly men from the council arrived. However, he became slightly anxious when they stood in the doorway, trapping him in the room with the snake, and told him that the snake catchers were on their way. Soon afterwards there was a tip tapping of high heeled shoes and two attractively dressed women appeared.

'The snake catchers are here,' announced one of the men.

Adrian peered past the women but, apart from a few onlookers from the other rooms, he couldn't see anyone who looked like a snake catcher.

The women spoke briskly to the two men who backed away gratefully. Then they took off their shoes and one of them tiptoed past Adrian to entice the snake from the boxes. The other woman, who was holding a big stick, watched carefully then hit the snake hard on its neck, killing it instantly. There was a cheer from the assembled company which the women acknowledged in a matter of fact way as they stepped back into their high heels.

Sandy was about to dispose of the snake when Gill said that she wanted to sketch its head. He shrugged and told her to be careful. Adrian helped Gill prop the snake's mouth open with a stick, then they both stood back as they saw its fangs were dripping venom into its huge black mouth.

'It's a beautiful specimen,' said Gill as they looked at the olive green scales on its back.

She settled herself at a safe distance and began to draw while Adrian asked Sandy to lend him a ruler. When he measured the snake it was almost two metres in length.

I wasn't sure how I felt about the story of the snake but it made me understand why our Batswana neighbours were fanatical about sweeping the area around their houses every day. The few people who had flower beds kept them small to discourage snakes from hiding in the undergrowth.

I followed this plan and when I decided to plant tomatoes I made sure that they were in a narrow south-facing bed. I was delighted when they started to bear fruit but was most upset to find that my precious plants were a delicacy for the flying black beetles that descended on them. Hearing the beetles chomping their jaws as they tucked into their evening meal was quite repulsive. I found that the only way to get rid of them was by chopping off their heads with a sharp pair of scissors. I took a fierce delight in this evening ritual, sometimes watched with squeals from Melinda and her friends. It was worth the effort and we were able to eat fresh tomatoes.

A more welcome visitor to our garden was a male weaver bird intent on building a nest worthy of a mate. South African weaver birds are about the same size as a British chaffinch but with more colourful plumage. Its chest and the back of the head is bright yellow while its back is a greenish yellow. This contrasts with its black beak and face and its beady red eyes.

Over a couple of evenings we watched our weaver bird building a nest in one of the trees in our garden. It collected twigs, grass and also leaves which it cut into strips with its beak.

'Good gracious!' said Adrian when he trained his binoculars on the bird. 'It's tying the grass into knots to bind the nest together.'

Melinda and Emily scurried about fetching grass which they put by the tree. When the nest was almost finished the bird chose the softer grass and hopped inside the bottom of the ball-shaped nest hanging from the tree.

'It's making a nice bed for the chicks,' I said.

When he had finished he fluttered his wings and chirped to attract a female to view the nest.

It wasn't long before a smaller weaver bird with a pinkish-brown beak came to check the nest. She pecked at the outside then hopped inside but came out quickly, uttering a series of chirps, then flew away.

'Will she come back?' asked Melinda.

Adrian shook his head. 'I don't think so.'

'Bird busy,' announced Emily.

We looked where she was pointing and, to our surprise, the weaver had already started on another nest.

For the next few days our bird's efforts to attract a mate were interesting to watch in the late afternoons. We were pleased when the fourth nest met with the approval of our bird's potential spouse and she hopped in to lay her eggs.

It would be good to report that we enjoyed watching the baby birds fly from the nest but that was not to be and we never found out why.

In the meantime, we had a lot to think about. Melinda celebrated her fifth birthday at the end of October with a small party for her friends. As well as home school I was increasingly involved with the Day Care Centre. In November we had an open afternoon for parents and YWCA members. The newly painted walls were covered with the children's work and they had learnt a variety of songs with actions which they sang with confidence. Everyone was most impressed and afterwards the number of children increased dramatically which was a mixed blessing.

Adrian was busy with teachers' courses and we had various colleagues of his staying overnight as well as offering hospitality to Ted's relatives who were visiting from England.

Hugh and Mmatsela were in the process of building their own house on the other side of Mochudi and we often spent time at weekends helping them.

However, the great excitement was preparing for my parents' visit at the beginning of December. We needed to buy a larger tent so that we could go camping with them. It still wasn't possible to buy a tent in Botswana so we had another trip to South Africa and were again shocked at how different it was from the freedom of Botswana.

We also decided to buy a Land Rover as our Nomad was becoming increasingly unreliable and we planned to travel a lot with my parents.

Chapter 12

Christmas, Gemstones and Tick Bites

Christmas was an important celebration in Botswana because it was the only time when the men who worked in South African mines came home to spend precious time with their families.

My parents had to travel further to celebrate Christmas with us and it was with much excitement that we drove to the airport on December 11th to pick them up in our newly purchased Land-Rover. Despite their long journey, they were wide awake and Dad was full of questions while Mum chatted to me with her granddaughters snuggled beside her.

'It's good to be back in Africa,' said Dad the next morning as we sat on the veranda making plans for their next six weeks.

'It will be different from your Christmas in Nigeria when Ramadan was the big celebration. And,' I said as I looked at the girls talking excitedly to their friends at the gate, 'there were no grandchildren then!'

Throughout their seven weeks stay the Batswana children were a backdrop to our life and Dad meticulously recorded their names in his diary along with a detailed description of each day's events.

Adrian wanted to show them some of the schools he visited but they had already broken up. The Day Care Centre had a shorter holiday and I said I would take Mum and Dad to visit after they had time to settle in.

In the meantime we were busy showing them Mochudi and introducing them to our friends. Heather and George were still living in a rondaval which fascinated Mum and Dad who made themselves quite at home when we visited.

When I introduced them to Beatrice at the Day Care Centre she said she needed to check her lands before her husband's homecoming and invited us to go with her and the twins. I said that we would pick them up the day after crèche closed.

'How would she get there if you weren't giving her a lift?' Dad asked as we drove to Beatrice's house.

'She'd have to wait till someone was going in that direction.'

I slowed down and Melinda waved to the twins who were waiting excitedly for us.

We drove along a bush road to Oliphants Drift then turned north along a very bumpy track until we came to a halt under a large acacia tree. In front of us was a small rondaval, a covered kitchen area and an area for threshing and winnowing.

Pleased to be out of the vehicle, the children ran around shouting and the twins took great delight in chasing the chickens. Melinda and Emily were more wary, especially of the cockerel strutting around.

Maize was growing immediately behind the rondaval and we followed Beatrice to investigate the crop. Some of the green stalks were almost as high as me with yellow cobs hanging in the centre of most of them.

'It is a good crop,' said Beatrice with satisfaction, 'but we must harvest soon in case we have a drought.'

She led the way through the lines of maize to beans growing in clumps on the other side. 'They are nearly ready.' Beatrice looked pleased as she bent down to pick one.

'Where do they get their energy from?' Mum murmured as the children rushed past brandishing sticks.

By this time the sun was beating down and I felt the beginning of a headache. Dad was asking Beatrice questions and I knew we could be there a long time.

'Come on kids,' I said, 'We'll go and find some drinks.'

We crouched in the shade of the acacia tree and I passed round drinks from the cool box. It revived the children and they went back to their earlier game of chasing the chickens.

The men returned with Beatrice holding a large water melon. She took it into the rondaval and came out with large pieces of melon and a bowl of water for us to wash our hands. It was more refreshing than a glass of water and I felt revived.

'Now I will prepare your chicken,' Beatrice said as she threw some grains down for the hens.

Mum looked at me enquiringly and I shrugged as I wondered, with some apprehension, what was going to happen next.

There was an angry clucking as Beatrice stalked one of the larger hens then grabbed its legs and carried it into the kitchen area. Mum gasped at the sound of terrified squawking followed by silence.

'Chicken dead' announced Emily.

I nodded and thought that if Beatrice planned to cook the chicken we would be there all afternoon. However, it was wrapped in newspaper when she presented it to Mum with a flourish.

'Thank you very much, it's very kind of you,' stammered Mum.

'I'll put it in the cool box,' I said.

A man arrived and greeted us in Setswana before speaking to Beatrice who nodded in agreement. She introduced him and announced that he wanted a lift as far as Pilane.

'No problem,' said Adrian.

The return journey with six adults and four children was somewhat squashed but we arrived safely and Dad had another adventure to write up in his diary.

Preparing for Christmas included several trips to Gaborone. There were also invitations to visit friends including Nora, Michael and Tina who had returned from leave.

Just before Christmas we had a short expedition to find a tree suitable to use as our Christmas tree. Bertha looked up in amazement when we brought in a spindly evergreen bush. She was even more surprised when we put it in a pot and proceeded to decorate it with homemade decorations as well as some we had brought from England.

Despite the excitement about having a break for Christmas, everyone was becoming increasingly concerned by the lack of rain and the persistent heat which affected us all. However, this changed on Christmas night when there was a violent storm with thunder and lightning. It woke up the donkey who again showed his displeasure by braying loudly. Amazingly, Melinda and Emily slept through it and were up early eager to open their presents. This included a small dolls house with miniature furniture which was a great success.

The sun came out as singers from the Zionist Christian Church passed on their way to worship. The rhythmic foot and hand clapping was fascinating and I found myself tapping my feet as well. Soon afterwards Itumeling, Tumo, Poppy and Cecilia arrived and admired the Christmas tree then sat on the floor and played with the dolls' house.

Mrs Motsawogle and another neighbour came for afternoon tea while the kids played outside. There was another sharp shower but, instead of taking cover, all the children ran about shouting 'Pula!' as they lifted up their open mouths to catch the raindrops.

However, the rain had stopped by the time our friends, four couples and their children, arrived for a buffet supper.

The highlight of my parents' trip was to be a camping holiday in the Okavango Delta. In preparation for this, we thought it would be a good idea to have a trial camp for two nights at Lake Bothoen, near Kanye. George and Heather had mentioned that they planned to visit their friends in Kanye and were delighted when we asked if they would like to join us on the journey. So, on 27th December, we set off with George and Heather squashed into our Land Rover as well as the six of us.

Skirting Gaborone we drove along a laterite track with sorghum and maize growing on either side. There was no sign of the Christmas rain and the land looked parched.

'I'm hot' announced Melinda.

'I think we all are,' said Adrian as he pulled off the road. There was little shade but the cold drinks helped ease our thirst. We were enchanted to see a blue cheeked bee-eater perched on a spindly bush amid tall grasses, its green and blue plumage iridescent in the sunshine.

Feeling refreshed, we continued along the Hunters Road which we had heard ran from Cape Town to Bulawayo. We followed a sign to Kolobeng pointing away from the main track.

Soon afterwards we came to the scattered foundations of some buildings and a monument in the shape of a pyramid. The inscription read: 'Here dwelt Dr Livingstone, Missionary and Explorer, 1846-1851'.

During that time, with the help of some of the local people, Livingstone built a church and began preaching. His wife, Mary, gave birth to their daughter, Elizabeth who died six weeks later. He and his family, as well as those living nearby, were forced to leave in 1851 when the settlement was raided by Boers from South Africa wanting more farmland. As a result the family embarked on a long trek north across the Kalahari.

Whether it was the heat or simply that he felt ambivalent about the price Livingstone's family paid for his missionary exploits, Dad showed little interest in the grave and its surroundings.

We drove past rocky outcrops keeping our eyes open for wildlife but all we saw was a dead iguana lying on the road so we stopped to have a good look. It was over one metre in length and its dark skin, sharp claws and scales protruding from its back made the girls slightly fearful.

'Touch it Minna!' squealed Emily as she backed away.

Melinda looked warily at Adrian who shook his head but bent down to point out the large eye at the side of its head.

We looked down to the valley below and saw a glint of water.

'There's the lake,' said George.

Our road wound past trees and bushes and then joined the road to Kanye before branching off towards Bathoen

Dam. There were a few other tents on the banks of the lake and we chose a spot with some shelter as well as a good view. As we were putting up our tents we saw a variety of birds including a sacred ibis wading in the shallows on its spindly legs and pecking for food with its long beak.

Dad passed his binoculars around so we could look more closely at the bird life then we gathered firewood from under some acacia trees nearby. According to Dad's diary I 'cooked a tasty stew over our wood fire which we sat around under a tropical moon.'

We had heard that this area was rich in semi-precious stones so the next day we decided to try some prospecting. When they retired Mum and Dad had set up a small business making gem stone jewellery and spent enjoyable trips to various beaches collecting suitable stones which they polished in a rock tumbler.

George and Heather's friend from Kanye had told us where there was amethyst near the lake so we set off to look. We found a spoil heap which was the remains of a test excavation undertaken some years previously but was deemed not sufficient to justify commercial exploitation. Mum and Dad were delighted to find a quantity of broken amethyst in a trench that had been part of the excavation so we set about picking out stones that they could use in their jewellery making. The children were keen to help and scurried about picking up whatever took their fancy. Altogether we collected about 20.1b

'That will keep us going for the next couple of seasons' said Mum with satisfaction.

The following day we dropped George and Heather at their friends in Kanye and continued to Malopwabojang which means River of Grass. We stopped to stretch our legs and the girls played hide and seek in the grass until Melinda ran back looking frightened.

'I've got a spider on me and it won't come off!' she wailed and held out her arm.

'That's not a spider, it's a tick,' said Adrian as he bent down to prise it off.

'Put cream on' announced Emily and stood on tiptoe to get a good view.

I was surprised to see Melinda's arm beginning to redden so I squirted some antiseptic cream into her hand and she gingerly rubbed it on her arm.

'You'll be better soon,' I said cheerfully.

But Adrian and Dad exchanged worried glances.

'We'd better check we haven't any ticks on our legs,' said Adrian before we got going.

Ticks were forgotten about when we stopped at the Cumberland Hotel in Lobatse and enjoyed tea on the veranda. However, according to my Dad's diary, we arrived home 'to an orgy of baths and de-ticking.'

The following week passed pleasantly and we were relieved we had no sign of tick bite fever.

New Year's Eve was the hottest day so far and even Mum and Dad's enthusiasm for new experiences was beginning to flag. Mmatsela and Hugh invited the girls to stay overnight in their new house. We, on the other hand, had a low key celebration and retired early to bed. However we had a rude awakening at midnight by the clanging of dustbin lids as all the kids who had been allowed to stay up came out and hammered them vigorously.

Everyone wished that the New Year would bring rain but, unbeknown to us, we were at the beginning of a seven year drought. By January 2nd the 1.00 pm temperature had reached 43°. We spent the day slowly getting everything packed for our big trip to the Okavango.

We were on the road by 7.00 am the following day. Adrian and I took it in turns to drive, with Dad taking an occasional turn at the wheel.

'Welcome to the Tropics!' I said as we stopped at the Tropic of Capricorn and unpacked breakfast from the cool box.

'It's a good road', Mum looked around approvingly as we continued our journey.

'You'd better make the most of it, there's hardly any tarred road after Palape.'

The heat was intense when we arrived in Francistown at 1.30 pm. We filled up with petrol, bought some take away food and stopped under a tree just outside the town. I started to hand out the food but none of us felt like eating. Melinda looked particularly unwell and had developed two nasty looking boils.

Adrian admitted he had a bad headache and we knew there was no way we could drive the next 490 km along a non-metalled road to Maun. By mutual consent we turned back to look for a camp site in Francistown and found a pleasantly situated site on a small farm. The owners were concerned when they saw the state we were in and suggested we were suffering from heat stroke. They directed us to a shady spot and said that they had been busy but now we were the only campers on the site.

'Let us know if there's anything you need, fresh milk in the morning or,' the farmer hesitated, 'we can recommend a doctor if you need one.'

We assured him we would be fine although looking at our flushed faces I realised we were far from fine. This was confirmed by the length of time it took us to erect the tent and unpack things we would need for the night.

After drinking copious amounts of cold water we rested in the shade while Melinda and Emily played listlessly with their dolls. Adrian slung a towel round his neck and went to have a shower. I was just nodding off to sleep in my chair when I realised that Adrian had been gone a long time so I went across to the shower and found him sitting on the floor with his eyes closed as the water sprayed down on him.

'Have I been here long?' he asked as he looked round in surprise.

'About 20 minutes.'

I picked up his sweat drenched clothes. He got up slowly, wrapped the towel round himself and we made our way back to the tent.

As we huddled in our small patch of shade the sky darkened and at about 1,000 ft we could see cascades of rain falling from black clouds.

'It's going to be a mighty storm,' said Dad.

I moved towards the tent then looked incredulously as the clouds evaporated leaving an almost straight vertical line in the glowing sky.

It was a surreal site and made one aware of how little control we had over the weather.

'The rain god must be elsewhere,' said Mum cryptically.

Having recently read Bessy Head's book, When Rain Clouds Gather, I was inclined to agree.

'Can I have a naartjie?' asked Melinda referring to the small South African orange that is sweet, juicy, easy to peel and a great favourite with children.

'You must have some water as well,' I said as I passed them round.

Feeling slightly refreshed we went for a walk round the farm. As well as cows they had chickens, a peacock, a rabbit with a broken leg and a couple of ponies. The owners' daughter offered to give the girls a ride and they enjoyed the thrill of their first horse ride.

We slept surprisingly well and had recovered from our dehydration by the following morning. However, we still had high temperatures and reluctantly decided to abandon our holiday in the Okavango and return to Mochudi in the cool of the evening.

Mum had a friend who had emigrated to Rhodesia and, although they rarely corresponded, she was keen to look across the border which was only 20 miles away. We took the road to Bulawayo but were stopped by police and told that they wanted to search us for weapons. The girls looked bewildered, Dad was genuinely worried but Mum regarded it as part of the adventure. Fortunately one of the policemen was from Mochudi so he and Adrian had a friendly chat. We turned round and did a tour of Francistown instead which didn't take long as it only had one main street at that time. It used to be a gold mining town and the railway line was an important link for transporting gold and other minerals to the coast. As well as several primary schools it had two secondary schools and a teacher training college. There was also a municipal swimming pool and after lunch we had a welcome swim before starting the long journey back to Mochudi, arriving home late on Saturday night.

We were hoping that we would recover when we were no longer travelling but, apart from Emily, we were still very unwell so I made an appointment for us to see a doctor in Gaborone on the Monday. We were unsurprised by the diagnosis of tick typhus and were pleased to come away with terramycin tablets and ointments to take. Unfortunately Mum also had flu and, whereas we recovered quickly once we had the correct medication, Mum took longer to recover.

'I go back to work next week, I don't think our trip to Maun will be possible,' Adrian said quietly to me one evening.

'I know, we'll have to think of something else but Mum desperately wants to see lions!'

'I don't think your Dad does!'

We laughed but I was sorry that the big adventure we had planned was no longer possible.

Chapter 13

A funeral, School visits and Limpopo Crocodiles

We saw less of Mmatsela and Hugh since they moved to their new house although Hugh sometimes called in after work. It was a surprise to see him as we were finishing breakfast the following morning.

'Is everything okay?' I asked.

Hugh shook his head and told us that one of Mmatsela's uncles had died the day before. As senior brother-in-law, it was his responsibility to organise the funeral.

'Had he been ill long?' asked Adrian after we had given our commiserations.

'He became ill at his cattle post and was taken to hospital where he died.'

'And when's the funeral?'

'Tomorrow at our house.'

We all gasped.

'That's cutting it fine,' observed Dad.

'It is rather but that's the custom.' Hugh turned to Adrian, 'I just called to invite you, as a friend of the family, to attend the funeral ceremony.'

'I'd be honoured,' said Adrian in surprise.

Hugh looked relieved. 'I've got to go now, his body will be arriving from the hospital at our house sometime this morning.'

'Will there be many mourners?' I asked.

'Probably about 200. They'll be arriving all day to keep vigil over the coffin.'

'But where will they sleep?' Mum looked shocked.

'They won't get much sleep although some of them will probably nod off somewhere outside our house.' Hugh looked at Adrian, 'It's okay, I don't expect you till the morning!'

Adrian left early the next morning. He arrived as an ox that had been slaughtered was boiling in large cast iron pots outside. Male members of the family were digging the grave, making sure it was deep so that wild animals would not be able to get in. Women were busy preparing maize porridge.

The ceremony was conducted by the local pastor and lasted over an hour with mourners adding their own contributions. After the burial and speeches the ox meat was distributed to the family and guests according to their status. Some sat on the ground but most people sat on chairs that had been hired for the occasion. A few of the older men had brought their kgotla chairs to sit on.

'How is Mmatsela?' I asked Adrian when he returned.

'Exhausted! It's a good thing they've only just moved there and so it didn't matter having so many people in their garden.'

It took Mum a week to fully recover from her bout of flu and by then Adrian was back at work. He thought it would be interesting for them to see some of the schools in his area.

The first school they visited was at Dikwididi, a village about 20 km south of Mochudi. Dikwididi is Setswana for tadpole and the village was named for the large number of tadpoles in the area which had increased as more boreholes were dug.

They parked under a huge marula tree that was shedding its fruit which is about the size of a plum. It makes a good local beer and there are stories of elephants liking the marula fruit so much that they gorge large quantities which ferment in their stomach and they become intoxicated.

Mum and Dad were welcomed by the headmaster who was happy for Mum to take photographs. This wasn't easy as the children were so excited they surged forward and Mum kept walking backwards as she attempted to get a good shot. She was impressed with the girls' green uniforms and neatly pleated skirts which were made by one of the teachers.

One of the boys showed them a model lorry he had made from pieces of wire and old beer cans for the wheels.

The next school they went to was at Modipane, a larger village close to the border with South Africa. The school was just below Rainsnake Mountain. Mr Molibatse, the young headmaster, told them that there were lots of baboons this side of the mountain. On the other side were leopards which hunted the baboons.

'Why is it called Rainsnake Mountain?' asked Mum who loved a good story.

Mr Milobatse told them two different versions of the legend of the mountain. Later, Dad recorded the stories in neat but almost illegible handwriting in his diary about their trip to Botswana.

Dad sometimes seemed bewildered by the number of people dropping by to see us. Our Ghanaian friends, Mary and Botchway, called one day and asked if I would look after the boys while they went shopping. Afterwards they invited us for a traditional Ghanaian meal and told Mum and Dad how nice it was to have friends who had lived in Ghana. They were about to be transferred to a school in another area which they weren't looking forward to. This was part of a government drive to open a lot more schools.

The rest of their holiday passed with trips to Gaborone, Matsieng's Footprints, Oodi Weavers and visits with friends. By the time they left, my parents had met them all including Martha from Tsabong and Wolfgang from Maun. Everyone was sorry to hear about our aborted trip to the Okavango and someone suggested we could see hippos at Buffels Drift on the Limpopo River which was much nearer.

Dad was thrilled at the idea of going to 'the banks of the great grey-green greasy Limpopo River all set about with fever trees' described by Rudyard Kipling in his story about the elephant's child who wanted to know what crocodiles ate for their dinner.

My mother enjoyed the trip so much that she wrote an account of it which she circulated to family and friends. Her account, written for friends and family, is copied below.

Limpopo Trip, January 1980
Hazel Williams

The highlight of our seven weeks holiday in Botswana was undoubtedly our three day camping trip to the Limpopo River. Eight of us left Mochudi about midday on Friday in two Landrovers: Heather, Adrian, the two children, Ray, myself and friends George and Heather. We were making for a place called Buffels Drift about 150 Km from here on the Limpopo River. We turned onto the old Francistown road just before the Tropic of Capricorn then took another turning onto a sandy bush road and headed towards the Transvaal border. We came to a locked gate across the road and could not persuade the gate boy to open up. He was convinced we wanted to cross into South Africa at the non-existent border post at Buffels. This might have been the end but 'Friend Heather' came to the rescue as she was able to speak enough Setswana to make the boy understand that we only wanted to look for game by the river. So, through and on we went, our eyes peeled for game until the front Landover gave the cry 'Ostrich!' At the same time the following Landrover had spotted wildebeest.

We were still game viewing when a truck pulled up alongside. Heather and Adrian recognised the driver as someone they had met at the Tropic some months before. He was a farmer in that area and offered to let us camp on his land. We must have followed him for about 15 Km well past Buffels Drift. When we arrived at his farmhouse we were all travel weary and thirsty and were delighted when his wife invited us for a cup of tea. He, their names were Theo and Verna Riggs, took us to a camp site by the Limpopo river. It was really lovely. There were tall shady trees, a pebble beach for Ray and I to go stone collecting, many lovely birds and the biggest thrill of all, crocodiles!

We set up camp, got a fire going and proceeded to barbeque eight T Bone Steaks. It was quite dark by this time but we had a gas lamp that stood on top of the Landrover and gave us a very good light. The children were good little campers. Melinda was a little afraid that the crocodiles would come out of the river in the night. The only thing that worried Emily was 'no food'. It must have been about 8.30.by this time and all we heard was 'meat Mama, meat'. After our lovely meal of T Bone Steaks, foil roasted-potatoes and onions we washed up, put the light out and sat round a glowing fire. The sky was midnight blue, and full of stars; the Southern Cross was very clear. There were also fire flies dancing about six feet above our heads. The children fell asleep by the fire and were carried into bed.

Saturday was a very exciting day. Theo had asked if the men would like to go buck shooting, as he needed meat to feed his workers. Whilst Ray bowed out, Adrian and George decided to try their hand. So, after breakfast our two intrepid hunters set off, accompanied by Friend Heather as an observer. They picked up two guns from the farm and a guide and we didn't see them again until late afternoon. The rest of us spent a very pleasant morning wandering by the river. At this point the river was running between high mud banks, broken by a wide stony beach on the Botswana side. The other side was the Transvaal and it was illegal to land on the other bank. There was a great deal of bright red jasper amongst the stones and we were able to bring about six lbs back with us.

We had our lunch in the camp and then sat in the shade for a while resting. It was extremely hot. After a while we heard grunting noises and there, a few yards away, was a wart hog family trotting along in the grass. There were four adults and six babies, making for the river to drink perhaps. There was also a hornbill feeding its young in a tree nearby. It spent the entire day flying backwards and forwards with food. About three p.m. we decided to go for a walk looking for game, Ray, Heather, myself and the two children. It was a great mistake as the sun was blazing down out of a

cloudless blue sky and very soon we felt like grease spots.
We were rewarded by seeing quite a few impala. We sat
down on a log to rest and Emily promptly went to sleep. I
wonder if any of you reading this account have ever carried
a sleeping 2½ year old half a mile in the hot African sun?
By the time I spotted George & Heather's orange tent the
sweat was running in rivulets down into my eyes and I very
thankfully deposited my youngest grand-daughter onto a
mattress where she went on peacefully sleeping. A cup of
tea was a great reviver and then Ray and I wandered off to
look down on the river from a higher part of the bank.

Imagine our delight when we saw three crocodiles
basking in the sun on the beach. We stood and watched them
for a while and I was about to go back for my camera when
we heard the hunters' Landrover coming back. The noise of
that disturbed them and they all slid into the river. Our two
young hunters arrived bloody but unbowed. Bloody,
because George's rifle had recoiled and cut his head just
above the eye, unbowed because Adrian had shot an impala
at 300 yards range which was a great achievement as he
had not fired a rifle since he was 12 years old. Theo was
very pleased as he felt a responsibility to his workers.

That was only half the excitement of the day. About six
o'clock Theo and Verna arrived with a small flat bottomed
boat to do some fishing. So, down to the Limpopo we all
went, cameras at the ready. The idea was to get the net right
across the river and tie it to the opposite bank. (Quite illegal
of course as it was a different country over there). Then the
fish would swim into it. Easier said than done. Ray was
stationed on the bank with a rope tied round a tree and he
had to let it out as required. The other three men got into
the boat with two large shovels as oars and started paddling
across the river with the net. Well it really needed a cine
camera to do justice to what happened next. The current
was a great deal stronger than it looked, and no way could
they get the boat across the river. They kept playing the net
out and getting swept further and further downstream while
Ray was desperately hanging on to the other end round the

tree. Theo then decided Adrian and George should change ends, and in so doing swamped the boat and got a far larger dose of the Limpopo than they had bargained for. The two Heathers and myself were running up and down the beach getting the best photos we could, Ray was still hanging on to the rope, Emily started to cry 'my daddy, my daddy' and Melinda was very upset crying 'come back daddy the crocodiles will get you'. Well they managed to swim to shallow water with the boat and beached it. Theo then decided they should swim across the river with the net and tie it to a tree on the other bank. As the thought of crocodiles didn't seem to bother him, Adrian and George couldn't very well chicken out. So off they went again (still in shoes, socks, shorts and shirts). Ray is still holding the rope round the tree, with blistered hands by this time I might add. They did manage to get the net across. At this point the river would be about 40 yards wide. Adrian told us afterwards he thought his last moment had come when his foot hit a submerged log. He gave it a vicious kick and decided it was only a log. After all that great effort the fish boycotted the net, I don't doubt they had all been thoroughly frightened by this time, the crocodiles as well. They eventually swam back across the river and Ray thankfully abandoned his role in the great Limpopo Fishing Expedition. Undaunted, Theo said he would take us to another stretch of river the next day and fish below the weir. Once again it was dark before we got our evening meal, but the fire stoker-uppers got busy and soon it was crackling away. Strange how one doesn't mind the taste of smoked tea by a camp fire.

Sunday was another action packed day. After breakfast of sorghum porridge we decided to take the Landrover and go game-spotting. George and Heather wandered off on their own, bird watching and identifying trees. We had not gone far when Adrian suggested that Ray and I would get a better view if we sat on the front of the Landrover, which we duly did and hoped we wouldn't go down too many deep ruts to throw us off. We again saw many impala, monkeys, wart hogs and Egyptian geese. At the end of the viewing session we arrived at the farmhouse to collect some fresh milk, still sitting on the front of the vehicle. As we drove up Theo greeted us with 'My, you've got a good seat, you must have great faith in your son-in-law' (which of course we have).

Everyone reading this narrative will know of our interest in stones. Apparently a friend of Verna & Theo's on the next farm had a collection of stones picked up from around the Limpopo area and also semi-precious stones from her father's mine in South West Africa. Would we like to go and see them? Would we? Of course we would! So off we went, inside the Landrover this time, to Basinghall Farm, about 8 miles away. It was a lovely place, and Alice Beamond greeted us like old friends. We had cups of coffee while we were looking through the collection. It seems as though her father's stone is tourmaline which is very beautiful when polished, we hope we may have made a business connection there.

Back at camp George and Heather were wondering what had happened to us and we found them at the farm when we got back. After a picnic lunch we began to strike camp as Theo and Verna were coming to take us fishing at the weir. We were just about packed up by the time they arrived and off we went.

It was again a lovely part of the river, greener than where we had been and flowing quite fast below the weir. Once again Ray was the tree man, while the other three men swam out across the river with the net. The current was very strong and they had difficulty in swimming across it. They managed to get the net across to the other bank and caught one very large fish. Theo brought the fish out and was about to go back and try for more when he quickly shouted to the others to come out and call it a day. Apparently he had seen the tracks of a very large crocodile that must have gone into the water just as we went down.

So that was just about the end of our Limpopo adventure. We drove up to the farm, where Verna gave us cups of tea. We exchanged addresses as they are coming to England for

three weeks in May. It will be their first visit to the U.K, so
we hope to be able to repay a little of their hospitality.

On the way back we stopped at Buffels Drift and had
drinks and biscuits by the river. It was very peaceful in the
evening sunlight and much wider there. I suppose the next
best thing to seeing a hippo, was to see its enormous
footprints as it had gone into the water. It would have made
a perfect weekend even more perfect if we could have seen
it! We got back to Mochudi about 10 pm, very tired, very
dusty, and very happy. We all agreed it had been a great
success.

The last week of Mum and Dad's holiday was spent visiting
friends who were nearly as sorry as we were to see them go.
They left on 28th January with their bags full of mementoes
and their heads full of memories.

Chapter 14

New challenges, Moshupa visit, Mochudi Farewells

We all felt a sense of loss after Mum and Dad's departure.

I was getting ready to take the girls to the Day Care Centre one morning when I heard Melinda say, 'I don't want to go to crèche, I want to stay with Granny.'

'Can't, gone home,' Emily replied.

'Where?'

'Up sky.'

I smiled as I pictured my parents riding on a white cloud as I tried to banish a feeling of homesickness.

Fortunately a surrogate Grandfather arrived when Hugh's father and brother came for a holiday away from a cold English winter as well as political unrest due to the Steelworkers strike. Hugh's father was delighted to be called Grandfather Joe and the name stuck even when the girls were older and he visited us at our home in England.

News of the refurbishment and new equipment at crèche had spread and 50 children enrolled at the beginning of the new term. This meant a lot of extra work for Beatrice and Miss Kgobe as well as myself and Sue. After writing to the committee I was pleased when I arrived at crèche to find a very pleasant cook/cleaner and a delighted Miss Kgobe.

As I drove home I started to think about other things I could do. I wondered about the possibility of teaching an evening class in Gaborone, little knowing that a decision was about to be made for me.

A few days later Adrian arrived back from a meeting with Bram Swallow smiling broadly.

'They want me to run TAPU!'

'The Teaching Aid Production Unit in Francistown?'

'Yes, there'll be more opportunities for you and there's an English Medium primary school Melinda can go to.'

'Gosh!' I wasn't sure how I felt about having to make new friends but it would solve the problem of Melinda's schooling and could lead to part-time work for me.

'When do you start?'

'It's not finalised yet but sometime before the current Danish co-ordinator leaves.'

'So what would the work involve?'

'Being in charge!' Adrian laughed. 'I went there once. They are part of the Curriculum Development Department and have printing and wood-work departments all under the same roof. They are meant to run workshops for teachers but I don't think they ever have.'

'You could certainly change that!'

'Yes!' Adrian began to outline some plans he had thought of as he drove back from his meeting with Bram.

Suddenly there was a scream and we ran outside to see Melinda lying under her bar. Unfortunately she had fallen into some thorns sprouting from the base of the tree where the bar was fixed so she was scratched as well as bruised, although not badly. Adrian carried her inside and we tacitly agreed that now was not the time to say that we would be moving. In fact, when we did tell her, she wanted to know if there would be a bar in our new garden and Adrian promised that there would be. Two months later, when we took possession of our Francistown house, I saw with relief that there were indeed two suitable trees in the garden.

The weather was mostly uncomfortably hot but one day there was a violent storm with large hailstones hammering on the tin roof of our house. The atmosphere was subdued when I arrived at crèche the next day and heard that a child had been killed by lightning while she was sitting with her parents in their unfinished house in the centre of Mochudi. The smartly dressed children were playing quietly and, with raised eyebrows, I looked questioningly at Beatrice.

Beatrice shook her head. 'She wasn't one of ours.'

It was a strange time, looking forward but at the same time cherishing what we had.

Sandy Grant had been asked to write a book for children explaining how the Botswana Government worked but he was too busy with the museum so he asked me if I would like to do it. It was interesting work and gave me something to focus on. One Friday I visited the parliament building in Gaborone. Adrian picked me up at lunch time and we were fascinated to see the car park full of MP's pick-up trucks, or bakkies as they were generally called, ready to go straight to their farms for the weekend. Many of them had seen better days but that didn't bother the MP's who were more concerned with getting to their lands and cattle posts than driving smart vehicles.

'Any post?' asked Adrian when he returned from a trip to Gaborone to sort out his transfer to Francistown the following month.

'An invitation from Mary and Bochway to stay with them in Moshupa.'

'That would be nice, it's near Kanye isn't it?'

'Yes, but I gather it's just a small village and Mary is missing Mochudi.'

'It will be good to visit that area again, we won't be going in that direction once we've moved.'

'No, we'll be able to go to Rhodesia or Zimbabwe as it will soon be called.' I was excited at the thought. 'Perhaps we can visit Mum's friend in Bulawayo, I wonder what she thinks of the changes.'

'Probably not a lot if she's been there since the 1940s,' said Adrian.

Melinda and Emily were looking forward to seeing their friends again and we set off one Friday afternoon. We drove south, by-passing Gaborone, then turned west.

'That looks a bit like Papane Hill,' I said as we drove towards a low hill rising from the plain. Goats were grazing in front of some thatched rondavals and women were pounding food for the evening meal.

We passed a small general dealer on the sandy main street and a few traders sitting cross-legged selling their wares. A fishy smell wafted into our car where a stallholder was holding up some fish which had probably been caught from one of the rivers running through Moshupa.

'Look at those rocks.' Adrian slowed down and pointed to an outcrop of red rocks balanced precariously on top of each other.

'Hopefully we can have a good look later,' I said.

We turned off the main road when we saw a sign to the Secondary School.

The staff houses were set back from the main school and the boys were playing by their open gate. They ran out in excitement and we pulled into their drive. Mary and Bochway welcomed us and soon the four children were playing happily.

'They are so pleased to see their friends again,' said Mary as we sat on their veranda watching them chasing each other round the garden. 'We are the only ex-pat family at the school.'

We told them about our move to Francistown and I said that they must visit us when we were settled there.

'We saw some amazing rock formations on our way in', said Adrian.

'No one can understand why the rocks don't fall with the way they are balanced. The superstition is that they only fall when the village chief is dying. We'll take you there tomorrow,' said Bochway.

There was a cry from the smallest boy who had fallen over but he quickly picked himself up and carried on running, waving a stick as he went.

'Do you think it will be safe for the children?' asked Mary anxiously.

'They'll enjoy running round the smaller rocks,' said Bochway. 'And we can take you to the river afterwards.'

After a delicious Ghanaian meal we were happy to go to bed early because we knew that the children would want to go outside and play as soon as it was light.

Sadly we didn't visit the rocks because Adrian woke up in the night with a stomach bug and was unwell for much of the day.

We left him resting and went for a walk in the village where we bought some sweets for the children. Fortunately they didn't feel like running around when we got back and the boys were happy to settle down and play with Melinda and Emily's dolls which had accompanied them on our journey.

While I helped Mary prepare lunch she told me how isolated she felt. The school was smaller than the secondary school in Mochudi and all the other teachers were Batswana.

'It seems very quiet, don't any of the teachers have children?' I asked.

'Some do, but people here often go to their lands at the weekends.'

I felt sorry for Mary and asked about her family in Ghana. As she talked, it brought back colourful memories of our year in Ghana as volunteer teachers 12 years previously. I could understand that it must be difficult for Mary adjusting to life in Botswana as Ghana did not have the historical connections with the country that Britain had.

By the afternoon Adrian was feeling much better and was keen to get on the road while he still felt able to drive. With promises to meet again we left, happy in the knowledge that we already had plans for supper with Mochudi friends that week.

George and Heather had moved from their tiny house and were now living near us. We made the most of their company while we could and our house continued to be a place where friends often dropped by at the end of the day.

Adrian carried on visiting schools. He and Ted were also busy running courses at the teacher's centre in the museum.

He had an overnight trip to Francistown by train to make arrangements for our move. As well as visiting TAPU, he went to see the house we would be living in when the current co-ordinator and his family returned to Denmark.

'Bent wanted to know whether we would like their family dog,' said Adrian on his return.

'But I don't like dogs!'

'That's what I said. Perhaps we should take Roger,' he joked as we watched Emily and Tumo trying to encourage the cat to eat out of their hands.

'Roger's still a bit feral. I've asked Mrs Motsewole if the children can give him some scraps after we've gone.'

'She'll miss you.'

'And I'll miss her. Oh! I forgot to tell you, she's invited us to go to her lands at Tlokweng.'

'That will be nice and the journey will be straightforward as it's just the other side of Gaborone. You're going to be busy before we leave.'

'Yes, there's going to be an event for us at crèche; I think I'll have to prepare a speech. I hope you'll be able to come.'

'I'll make sure I can.'

As things turned out, Adrian wasn't able to come to the lands or to the farewell event at crèche as Bram wanted him in Francistown so there was enough time for a proper handover at TAPU before Bent left. He was excited about the challenge but wasn't looking forward to spending three weeks in a hotel instead of with us.

Everyone at the Day Care Centre was sorry we were leaving. In her speech of thanks, the chairwoman of the YWCA said I must thank my husband for allowing me do all the things for them that I had!

Letter to my parents when Adrian was in Francistown.

I now qualify for my 'bush drivers' certificate! Yesterday the girls and I went with Mrs Motsewole and her children to her new house in Tlokweng and then to her lands near the South African border. The grass was at least three feet high most of the way and it was difficult to see the track. I did a daring 18 km per hour most of the way. We didn't stay long as she doesn't have a compound at the lands but we wandered through a mealie field which towered above our heads. I asked if she knew where she was and was a little perturbed when she replied. 'No, it's like a forest isn't it'. We had lunch at her house in Tlokweng and returned to Mochudi in the afternoon.'

When we visited Michael and Nora at the secondary school they told us that the Rhodesian teachers there were very excited about the outcome of the election as most of them are Mugabe supporters. It was interesting listening to Radio South Africa afterwards because they were amazed by his victory especially as they had poured so much money behind Muzorewa. We hope we'll be able to visit the Victoria Falls with you sometime.

I'm going to have an article published in the World Education Service journal. I wrote about our trip round the Kalahari from the angle of while other five year olds were starting school ours were preparing to cross the Kalahari due to the flexibility of the WES scheme. I am, of course, delighted to be published but also rather relieved not to be home schooling when we are in Francistown.

It's strange to think that the next letter I write will be from Francistown. It was sad saying good-by to Adrian at Pilane station. The girls were very upset whereas for me, the sadness was mixed with excitement that a new chapter is about to begin.

Chapter 15

To Francistown by Train

Adrian's letter describing the journey 4th March 1979

Although I wasn't starting my job at TAPU until the end of the month, I had been asked to give a talk to primary school teachers on a science topic. My luggage consisted of a briefcase, three boxes of demonstration equipment and a holdall. Heather and the girls took me to Pilane Junction to catch the train which started in Mafeking and travelled through Botswana to Bulawayo.

It was dark when we arrived at the station half an hour before the train was due. Six people had just been dropped off and a small crowd was singing. Poor Melinda was very sad, very tired and was weeping rather loudly. Rather than wait for the train to arrive, we agreed it would be best for Heather to take the girls home.

I carried my bags to the north end of the platform to be near the first class compartments and sat on my holdall to wait. It was peaceful listening to people chattering, crickets chirruping and the occasional car passing over the railway line. Out of the quiet a single person starting singing a plaintive song, then two, then three, then six stood up and shuffled round dancing in time to the song. Others joined the dance, harmonising for a round or two then dropped out and others took their turn. Everyone seemed to appreciate the singing, the night stars and the crescent moon. The Southern Cross appeared to be pointing to where the train would come from, with Orion directly above us overseeing the whole operation.

Gradually people, thinking we were in for a long wait, settled down wrapping themselves in blankets with their drinks of milk, guava juice, beer or water. The night was warm so I sat in my short sleeved shirt and slacks watching, listening and thinking.

What a gratifying job I have. I can use a large amount of the odds and ends I've been picking up all my life as well as the ideas I've gained at University and Nigeria doing things I like in a very pleasant country with very warm genuine people. I do hope that my contribution is good enough.

As I listened I realised there were different languages being spoken. I suppose there were Rhodesian as well as different Botswana tribes. A group of Herero women were unmistakeable by their dress. They wear clothes in the style of their German colonisers – large skirts to the ground with many petticoats. Their head wear is tied in such a way as to resemble the horns of a bullock.

The train arrived at 8.30 pm. It was on time which was a good sign as the meeting starts at 8.30 am and the train is scheduled to arrive at 7.00 am. There was a mad dash to get on and then I had a clumsy walk down the corridor looking for first class and an empty compartment. I found first class but failed to find an empty compartment so ventured into second class sleeping six to a compartment. There are also third and fourth class sitting and perhaps standing. I was two carriages down from the front when I met the conductor who, seeing the struggle I was having with my belongings, said there was an empty second class half carriage that I could have on my own or walk to the back of the train for a shared first class. I opted for the second class and hired my bedding for the night. The railway in Botswana is owned and run by Rhodesia so I suppose travelling on it is sanction busting! The last train was several hours late because it was shot at on the way from Bulawayo and some compartments have bullet holes to prove it. The border town is about 50 miles north of Francistown for which I'm heartily glad.

It's a single track line so there are quite a few stops when the noise of the crickets takes over from the rumbling of the wheels to allow other trains to pass. The trains have a very large searchlight in front which lights up a great stretch of

107

track as well as the bush on either side. A moth, attracted by the bright light, flies in while the train is stationary and lands on the page I am writing on and deposits its mark. Mosquitoes buzz around then buzz off. I expect they are looking over the menu before settling down for a meal.

The train moves on. Thorn trees and marula trees are silhouetted against the light from the first quarter of the moon. There are no town lights in the distance, no lights of cars rushing along roads. The main road runs parallel with the railway but it is almost deserted at night, even more so than during the day. I drove up to Francistown two weeks ago; I overtook four cars and was overtaken twice in 400 km. When I drove back nothing overtook me.

We pass a wind pump whirring round and pumping water into a header tank from a borehole. The water was used solely for the steam engines but now is also used to water the cattle trains and troughs at the side of the track.

An hour from Pilane and nothing by which I can recognise where we are. Orion has moved to the west or, more correctly, I have moved to the east. Then looming out of the trees is Artesia or Mosomane as it's now called. It is an important watering stop and centre where railway workers live. Their small unlit corrugated tin huts (insulated with fibre glass) with small fires burning outside contrast with the well-lit brick built residence of the station manager. His garden is neatly kept with white washed stones along the path (or is it moonlight). The road is close to the track and on the far side is an empty bar with doors agape and curtainless windows allowing music from the radio to escape.

No one gets on or off. Carriage lights blink off as people settle down for the night. There must be water here as toads and frogs join in the night chorus.

A chance to study the moon carefully shows that, even though it is only in its first quarter, the whole of the moon can be seen. The sky is a deep dark blue-black with a single cloud close to the moon. The Milky Way clustering around *the Southern Cross spreads north over the train. I settle down to sleep.*

The train trundles on with frequent stops. I wake at Mahalapye, a large town with a lot of sidings. People get off and people get on. The next thing I know is we stop again and the sky is a dull grey and the acacia thorn a yellow-green. Gradually the sky lightens, the wispy clouds turn pink then white as the sun rises. It's very cold so I close the window and get up.

Feeling hungry, I wander along to the restaurant car. Breakfast won't be served till Francistown but morning tea will be served soon. I wander back to my compartment and glance at my watch; it's 6.30 am so I eat a few biscuits.

Shashe station at 8.00 am and the train is surrounded by people selling carved wooden impala, clubs and walking sticks at low prices. The white station guard, in his Rhodesian Railways uniform, cycles up to the engine to chat with the driver then cycles off again. A south bound goods train passes carrying copper from Zambia.

Shashe Dam comes into view as we cross the sandy Shashe river bed. The dam stores water for drinking and irrigation.

We pass fields of sorghum, some healthy and full of grain while some are almost withered. The rains are so unpredictable that fields next to each other can have different rainfalls.

Suddenly we reach Francistown where the next challenge awaits.

Flash Forward
Alyrene Neo

Alyrene Neo

It was February 1983 and I was looking forward to joining Adrian in Kasane 500 km north of Francistown near the Zambian border. This was the first teachers' workshop we had done together since I began working for the Curriculum Development Department six months earlier.

I got a lift with a young Dutch volunteer whose car was old and not particularly comfortable. The tarred road ended soon after Francistown and the driver's lack of experience on this type of road began to show. He was anxious to reach our destination and drove faster than was suitable on the rutted road. I clutched my stomach as he lurched sideways to avoid a fallen branch.

'Did you know I'm pregnant!' I gasped.

'Pregnant!' he looked horrified and slammed on the brakes.

'I'll be fine', I gulped as I was almost jolted off my seat.

From there on he drove carefully, occasionally casting worried glances in my direction.

I drifted off to sleep and woke up to find we had stopped. A camera clicked and I saw my Dutch friend photographing a group of elephants strolling across the road. He looked at me and grinned. A baby elephant was hurrying across the road with its mother behind guiding it with her trunk.

'She's a good mother,' I murmured as I realised we had reached the edge of Chobe Game Park.

The sun had already set by the time we arrived at the hotel overlooking the Chobe River.

As I got out of the vehicle I was assailed by loud croaking from numerous frogs. Then I heard a shout and Adrian ran towards me. After checking that the Dutchman had accommodation with another volunteer, we thanked him and settled down to enjoy the evening.

Adrian told me that my workshop would be the following afternoon and he had planned for us to go on a river trip in the evening. Hendrix, the TAPU driver, would take me back to Francistown after the morning break on Wednesday.

My workshop on how to teach the new Social Studies Syllabus was well received by the sixty or so teachers present and I looked forward to talking to some of the participants informally afterwards.

Unfortunately there was a logistical problem regarding the government vehicle and, for reasons outside my control, I found myself on my way back to Francistown at four o'clock immediately after the workshop finished.

'Will you go on the river trip?' I asked Adrian as we said goodbye.

He shook his head. 'Not without you.'

Hendrix was a careful driver and I relaxed in the comfortable front seat of the Ford 250 truck. As we drove through the darkness I thought of all the things Melinda and Emily had seen and how much more lay in store for them to share with their baby brother or sister. They had been delighted when we broke the news and busily suggested names.

Adrian didn't mind as long as he or she was called Neo which is Setswana for Gift.

Alyrene Neo was born five months later and our family of five was complete.

Part Two
Francistown

Christmas at T62

Chapter 16

T62, Chickens, Neighbours and TAPU

We moved from Mochudi to Francistown on March 25 1980. Melinda was five and Emily two and a half.

Our house was on the edge of the Government Housing area opposite smaller 'low cost' houses.

'Look! It says T62!' said Melinda who had jumped out of the car with me when we stopped to open the gate.

Bougainvillea trailed along the wire fence, its red petals providing a spot of colour in the overgrown garden.

Instead of a garage there was a car port. While we were unloading, the girls were excited to find a swimming pool at the side of the house where frogs had taken up residence. I was relieved to see it was empty and, although we never filled it, they enjoyed playing there after we had removed the frogs.

Inside, the house was similar to the one we had left with a small kitchen, dining room, large living room, bathroom, separate toilet and three bedrooms.

The back garden was bigger and backed onto other government houses, although they were mainly obscured by vegetation including elephant grass which threatened to take over. There was a neem tree with bright green foliage and two lemon trees laden with fruit. In the bottom corner was a sleeping room and a toilet which was a steward's quarter similar to the one we had in Nigeria.

However, what really took us by surprise was a rickety three tier construction which housed 27 chickens. We were greeted by a loud squawking as we looked in amazement at the hen house which was roughly made with old bits of wood tied together with twine.

'He said he'd sold them,' gasped Adrian, referring to the previous Teaching Aid Production co-ordinator as we were assaulted by the noise and smell of hens.

The chicken 'house' was almost three times Emily's height. She stood with her face upturned looking with interest at Melinda attempting to stroke one of the hapless hens.

'Good job we like eggs,' I muttered.

'We can make lemon curd,' added Adrian glancing at the lemon trees.

We laughed, slightly hysterically. As it turned out, we did make lemon curd and, after Adrian had fixed the structure, neighbours were happy to buy fresh eggs until we decided to give the hens away.

The following day I heard barking in the front garden and followed the girls out to investigate. I was met by a tall blond-haired man holding a russet coloured dog on a lead. I didn't know much about dogs but I could see it was a mongrel with the body of a labrador and the legs of a corgi.

'Adrian's at TAPU; I thought you'd already left,' I said frowning slightly at the outgoing co-ordinator.

'We leave this afternoon. But, there's a problem with the dog, the new owners can't have him till Monday, can you keep him till then?'

Melinda was already stroking the dog which was wagging its tale vigorously.

'I can see he's in good hands, aren't you Klump?' He smiled at the girls and began walking towards the gate. The dog barked but didn't follow him. However, I did.

'Who are the new owners?' I asked.

'I've told them your names, they know where to find you. Thanks, you're a star,' he said and walked swiftly away.

'We've got a dog!' shouted Melinda when Adrian arrived back from TAPU.

'He's not staying, someone's coming to collect him on Monday,' I warned.

'From what I've seen at TAPU, I wouldn't believe anything he says. Anyway it'll be fun to have a dog.'

Adrian was too busy patting Klump to see my raised eyebrows.

When I opened the front door the next morning there seemed to be something missing. I frowned slightly as I looked at the empty street and realised I couldn't hear voices. I had become used to children's voices as a backdrop to our life in Mochudi and the comparative silence was unexpected. The new houses opposite were not yet occupied. Behind them was the occasional noise from traffic on the road to Bulawayo. It would be another two weeks before Rhodesia became independent and vehicles of all descriptions would travel the road to and from Zimbabwe.

After Adrian left for work I sat on the veranda with a cup of coffee. I was missing Mmatsela who had been such a good friend with her help and advice when we arrived in Mochudi. Among other things she had introduced us to Bertha who Emily was already missing and I knew I should look for help in the house.

A noticed a young woman walking along the road and she paused when she saw me.

'Dumela Mma!' she called and slowly opened the gate.

'Dumela,' I replied as I wondered who she was.

When she reached the veranda she introduced herself as Tiny and said she was looking for cleaning work.

She was smartly dressed and said that her previous employers had returned to Europe.

'My employers also had children,' said Tiny when Melinda and Emily stopped running after Klump and stared at her.

I knew it would be difficult to find a replacement for Bertha but Tiny's English was good and I was relieved when she said she could start work the next day.

'What are we doing today?' asked Melinda when Tiny had gone.

'There's still some unpacking to do. You must decide where you want to put your toys.'

'But there's no one to play with,' complained Melinda.

'There's Klump,' I said as he bounded onto the veranda. 'Till his new owners collect him.' I added quickly.

'I hope they forget to come.' Melinda bent down and patted the dog.

We got on well with the couple in the house at the bottom of the garden. Ken was originally from Mauritius, an island in the Indian Ocean, and Lorraine was a 'Cape Coloured' South African. Life as a mixed race couple in South Africa was difficult and they left for Botswana. They were surprised, then pleased, when we invited them for coffee. Ken was an amateur radio enthusiast and I found it fascinating when he told us about different connections he had made. We were chatting over the fence one evening when he told us about a distressing conversation he had tuned into from Portuguese East Africa, which was to become Mozambique five years later. It was from one group of independence fighters to another saying they couldn't hold off the enemy much longer.

Adrian had always been interested in ham radio, but it was our daughter, Alyrene, who followed up his interest when she was working at a radio station in Uganda many years later.

We were looking forward to Mmatsela and Hugh's visit at Easter, but they were unable to come at the last minute. Instead we met up with the Russells, an English family who had recently arrived. Tony taught science at the secondary school; he and Ines had two boys, seven year old Martin and three year old Adam.

There was a children's film at the Club every Friday evening and our two families went together to see Star Trek. I described the event in a letter to my parents in which I said that it was a good thing that Melinda was tasting some of the 'delights of civilisation' as she had got rather out of touch.

She was terribly excited about going and, as we took our seats, she said loudly, 'Are these moving pictures?'

Later, when Spock unexpectedly went into a clinch with a beautiful alien, Melinda's clear voice rang out in horror: 'What's he doing, Mummy?'

That provided more laughs from the audience than the film!

At the end of our road there was a small rocky hill called a kopje, and we took the girls to investigate. It didn't take us long to scramble to the top and we visited it regularly. As I was pointing out things in the distance, I found myself missing the higher Papane Hill near our house in Mochudi with its magnificent views over the valley to the hill on the other side of town.

The kopje was so near our house that I didn't have a problem with the girls going there with Martin and Adam when Ines was at a prayer meeting. Like many children of our generation, Adrian and I had been brought up with a considerable amount of freedom to roam our local area. I would watch the children scamper down the road and usually met them at the foot of the kopje not long afterwards.

One time an elderly man was talking to them when I arrived. Martin looked slightly defiant, Adam was nonplussed but Melinda and Emily seemed worried.

'Dumela Mma,' the man said and held his right hand to his chest in greeting.

'Dumela Rra,' I replied.

He spoke softly, 'I am telling these children it is not safe here.' He paused, 'A big snake lives here.' Frowning slightly he looked at Emily; 'She is small, your little one. This snake can eat a small goat.'

I gasped and he nodded sadly.

'It is because the new houses take away their hunting areas.'

'I understand, thank you for telling me. Come along children.'

Emily held my hand tightly and my legs felt like jelly as we walked the short distance back to T62.

The girls were keen to see where Adrian worked and soon after we arrived he took us to TAPU. It was situated next to the Teacher Training College and near the English Medium primary school.

TAPU, employed 12 men and women who made a variety of teaching aids from wood and metal as well as printing booklets. There was a courtyard in the centre of the unit with buildings on both sides. Adrian shared his office with his secretary Melody; it was a small room in the building housing the printing department. Opposite the office was a dark room which was used to make plates for the printing machine.

'Why is it dark in here?' asked Melinda as we peered in.

'It needs to be dark for making photos,' Adrian told her.

After he was established at TAPU he sometimes took the girls there to develop and print our own black and white photos which were a valuable record of our time in Botswana.

In the courtyard was parking for the five-ton truck and a wood store. On the other side there was a covered area for wood and metal work and two store rooms. Later, when TAPU's future was secure, a room for teacher training and two more offices were put up.

Elijah was in charge of the printing department and was respected by the other workers. He told Adrian about a job that wasn't possible to do because the machinery wasn't working properly and suggested he got in touch with the Government Printer in Gaborone.

'I'll go tomorrow.' Adrian was keen to make necessary improvements straight away.

'Me go too,' said Emily as she and Melinda waved frantically as we stood on the station platform watching the overnight train disappear.

'We'll go soon.' I sighed as I realised that Adrian would still need regular trips to Gaborone which, instead of 45 km from Mochudi was over 400 km from Francistown.

On his return Adrian told me about the difficult encounter he had had with the head of the Government

Printing Department. He said that he had been aback when, after introducing himself, the manager pointed to the door and told him he wasn't welcome. Apparently they refused to work with TAPU due to clashes with the outgoing co-ordinator. Adrian knew that books were key to children's learning and that TAPU's current equipment and staff skills were insufficient to produce large numbers of teaching materials. He explained that repairing the printing machines was not something his staff were trained to do and asked if the Government Printing Department would be able to help with training the operators to a higher standard. Nearly two hours later he left with assurances of their help.

Adrian went straight to report the news to his boss, Jake Swartland, who was the head of the Curriculum Development team. Mr Swartland shook him by the hand and congratulated him on repairing relations between the two organisations.

When he returned, Adrian told me that Jake had said that this made the prospect of TAPU being closed considerably less. This was a relief because he had originally been appointed to close TAPU down, a fact that we were choosing to ignore. He knew he did not have long to prove that, not only was it viable, but was necessary to Botswana's plans for rapid expansion of primary education.

Flash Forward

When we visited Francistown in 2005 with Emily and her husband we were welcomed by Elijah, Melody and others who were keen to show us that TAPU was still thriving.

Chapter 17

Granny Helen in Francistown, Zimbabwe and Mochudi

We had just over a month to settle into our new life before Adrian's mother arrived. My mother-in-law was a larger than life character who was liable to exaggeration. She was slender and wore her hair in an elegant chignon. She claimed that she wore earrings because they made her look taller. Her nails were always carefully polished and she had sapphire and ruby rings on her fingers. Helen chose her clothes carefully and no one would know that most of them were bought from the local Oxfam shop.

Helen wrote the following account in Francistown after our trip to Zimbabwe three weeks after it became independent.

Heather and the girls met me at Gaborone Airport. They had hired a car and we drove to the Holiday Inn. It was late afternoon by the time we arrived. Our room opened onto gardens with a swimming pool so the girls were able to play outside. We decided to have an early night as we were all tired; Heather, Melinda and Emily had travelled by train from Francistown.

Breakfast was served in our room then the girls went to the pool. Melinda can really swim now. For lunch we had a cold meat platter with six different salads. We got a taxi to the station to get the overnight train to Francistown. The station was packed solid; Heather had booked our compartment but had to join the queue to give our names to the guard. She went to the front and people shouted, 'We were here first!' Heather said 'I've got an old lady and two children with me'! They all cheered and said 'You win!' We had a four berth compartment and the girls enjoyed having a top bunk each. The guard served coffee, made up our beds and I woke just before Francistown.

Adrian and his driver met us. This house is a dream. Heather has a very nice girl who does all the housework, my clothes are washed and ironed and put back in the bedroom each day. In the evening Adrian, Melinda and I went to watch traditional African dancing. It was wonderful sitting under the stars listening to drums, Mars and Jupiter so clear. On Saturday night Heather and I went to a party given by a Greek family in their garden. There were 50 chickens being spit roasted as well as steaks and lamb chops. We enjoyed the Greek music and dancing.

A few days later we set off on safari. First stop was the Zimbabwe border. I was the first woman from Lincolnshire to cross into the new independent country. We spent the first night at Greys Inn in Bulawayo. As soon as we arrived coffee was served by the swimming pool. The Zimbabwe people are so happy to be independent but the whites are very afraid for their future.

The next day we started the long journey to Victoria Falls. Only 12 weeks ago one had to travel in convoy and we saw many houses damaged and deserted. When we were about a mile from the falls we could hear the roar of the water. We stayed at the Victoria Falls motel and had a beautiful meal. Heather and I had chateaubriand and the children loved watching it being cooked at the table. Then we drove for a quick look at the Falls. Oh the roar of the water and the beauty! We were up early the next day and did a complete tour of them. We walked over three miles through rain forest and got soaked, the spray rises 2,000 ft and can be seen for 60 miles. No words or photos can describe the wonder of them, they are twice as high and two and a half times longer than Niagara Falls.

In the evening we went for a cruise down the Zambesi River. It was so romantic and beautiful. The captain let Melinda take the wheel, she was so thrilled and proud. Free drinks were served all the way, Adrian and I tried to drink our fare. We stayed on the top deck and the stewards filled our glasses as soon as they emptied. We saw fish eagles and many other birds.

When I woke up I saw a monkey sitting on the roof of the motel. We went for another look at the Falls then on to a crocodile farm. Some were only one year old but others were over ten years. Melinda was allowed to hold a tiny one in her hand but it bit her.

The next day we set out for Wankie National Park. Adrian had booked a lodge there, ours was called Impala Lodge. It was beautifully furnished with two large bedrooms, dining room, kitchen, sun lounge, bathroom and shower room. We had to provide our own food but there was a servant there who did all the work, I really liked being idle and waited on.

We visited all the main pans and viewing platforms in the area around Main Camp. The first thing we saw were giraffe then a zebra stood in front of the car and then herds of zebra, warthogs, sable, gemsbok, waterbuck, wildebeest, kudu, impala, reedbuck, duiker, steenbok, wild cat, side stripe jackal, black back jackal, bat eared fox, crocodile, banded mongoose. The furthest pan was 80 km away. While watching a giraffe drinking I crept down from the hide and stood to have a snap taken.

By the second day we kept saying, 'Wonder when we'll see elephants?' Suddenly Heather shouted 'There's one!' Over 80 passed in front of the car, we looked around and another 20 at the back of us. We watched them drinking and bathing then throwing sand over themselves. We left before they did as Adrian didn't fancy them pushing the car over. We then decided to go to another hide but were held up by a huge family of baboons; one mother had a tiny baby and the girls wanted to take it home but we didn't dare get out of the car because the Big Daddy one looked so fierce. It was ages before they let us pass. We hadn't been long at the next hide when 50 more elephants came to drink. The wind was blowing away from them so I left the hide and stood near them for a photo which Adrian took from the car. I had my back to them and Melinda shouted, 'The big one is *chasing you!' You never saw a 67 year old granny jump into a car so fast.*

We all hated leaving, had a good journey back, a lovely meal at Bulawayo, then back through the border to Botswana. The children were just perfect the whole time.

Tomorrow we set off to Mochudi for two days. Then I begin my long trip back to England. I had to write this all down so I will know it has not been just a beautiful dream.

We were shocked when we got back, tired after the long journey, to find that our house had been burgled. The living room was strewn with our possessions and, to our disgust, there was faeces in one corner. Fortunately, apart from Adrian's overcoat, none of our clothes or children's toys had been taken. I was disappointed about losing some CDs but the other items were replaceable although not all of them could be bought in Francistown. The things taken were a pillow, sleeping bag, beer, sherry, Weetabix, eggs, soap powder, bubble bath and face toner. Looking back all these years later, it reads like a list of items for a rough sleeper but at that time we were new to the idea of city life and the poverty that often came with it. In fact, apart from a stolen bicycle, it was the only problem of theft we had during our five years in Francistown. Tiny told us she had notified the police who had taken finger prints but the thieves were never found.

Emily, in particular, was looking forward to staying in Mochudi when we took Granny Helen to the airport. She hadn't been able to understand why we were in Zimbabwe and kept asking, 'When we going to Mochudi?'

However, she was excited to see Nora and Tina briefly at Francistown airport. Nora was expecting a baby and they were flying to England where Michael would join them later. In those days there were no rules about people standing on the tarmac to greet or send off friends and family.

Adrian had TAPU business to do in Gaborone so he went by train the day before us. He had arranged for the TAPU driver to take us to Mochudi in our car. George and Heather's new house was big enough for us all to stay and it was good to introduce Adrian's mother to our friends. As soon as they heard we were in Mochudi, Poppi, Cecilia and the rest of the gang ran from their houses to join us in Heather and George's garden. They had invited Mmatsela and Hugh for supper and also Michael who was on his own since Nora and Tina's departure to England.

The following day, when Adrian was in Gaborone, we went to Crèche. Everyone welcomed us and the children sang songs for Granny Helen. Afterwards we drove to the museum and Helen loved the view over Mochudi. On the way back we called on Sue at the Secondary School who told me how much her four year old daughter missed Melinda. She said that she actually had to take them to our house to prove we were no longer living there.

'My bus!' shouted Emily in delight as we drove past Poppi's father's bus on our way back to George and Heather. Assured of their welcome the children ran after us and took up their game where they had left off the day before.

We were all sad to see Helen leave the following day when we said goodbye to her at the airport. She promised to phone my parents as soon as she got back and I knew that Adrian's father, in his gruff way, would want to hear every detail.

Chapter 18

New Opportunities, Klump and Seretse Khama

Francistown was founded in 1897 near the Monarch gold mine and named after Daniel Francis, an English prospector from Liverpool. As a result Francistown was the largest town in what was then Bechuanaland. When mining was no longer viable it became a centre for recruiting miners from the surrounding countries who were then transported to South Africa by railway. By 1980 Francistown had expanded and there were three secondary schools and a primary school in each ward.

Adrian told Elijah about the work I had done at Mochudi Day Care Centre. He like, the rest of the TAPU staff, lived with his family in one of the Francistown wards. Elijah was aware of the benefits for his ward if there was a centre there similar to the one in Mochudi, so he invited us to visit one afternoon. Organising another crèche had not been on my mind when we moved to Francistown. However, the girls and I arrived at TAPU at the appointed time and we set off with Adrian and Elijah to meet his family.

Unlike the government housing area, none of the roads were tarred but they were straight with single story houses on either side. The local government had just provided toilets opposite the houses but had not yet enclosed them. When Adrian joked about it to Elijah he said that most people used the facilities after dark.

It was good to meet Elijah's wife and his well-behaved children but I realised that the situation was very different to Mochudi where the crèche had been established by the YWCA who were ultimately responsible for the running of it.

'What do you think about Elijah's suggestion?' asked Adrian later that evening.

I shook my head. 'The girls are settled at nursery in the mornings and anyway I want to continue the research I did in Nigeria into pregnancy and childbirth practises.'

'I thought you'd say that. And what about that book you wanted to write?'

'I plan to start by writing magazine articles. It's a pity there's no independent newspaper in Botswana, I've always wanted to be a journalist.'

I had been in touch with Dr Van de Meuler who was a gynaecologist at the hospital. He sounded interested in my research project and introduced me to Mrs Dagwe, the sister in charge of the Maternity and Child Health unit. She invited me to her house the following week and I was looking forward to going. However I hadn't bargained on Klump coming too.

'Go home! You're not invited,' I said but he just wagged his tail and bounded along in front, occasionally stopping to sniff something that took his fancy.

Mrs Dagwe was surprised to see the dog, but presumably put it down to the fact I was English. I didn't like to admit I had no control over the animal and wasn't even a dog-lover. Fortunately he was well behaved and sat quietly on my feet, which felt rather squashed by the end of the visit.

I gave Mrs Dagwe a copy of my article, Pregnancy and Childbirth among the Gude, which had been published in the Midwives Chronicle the previous year and she said she looked forward to helping me.

After meeting a local midwife, I realised that there was little comparison with the remote Mandara Mountains where we lived in North East Nigeria. However, there were still traditional midwives in some Botswana villages. After a baby was delivered the afterbirth was buried in the hut where the child was born. As so many men worked away for most of the year, children born out of wedlock were an accepted fact of life. The midwife I spoke to said that it was important for women to have children to look after them in old age.

Klump continued to be an embarrassment. He was fine around children but considered it his duty to protect us from random visitors. We had invited a Ghanaian couple for supper. As this was mid-winter it got dark early and when five Ghanaians turned up, instead of the two we had been expecting, I had difficulty recognising them. Sensing my hesitation Klump barked and growled menacingly so that the ladies in the party ran screaming to the gate. In my anxiety to retrieve the dog I skidded on the veranda and landed at the gentlemen's feet. Finally I managed to get hold of Klump's collar and pull him into the kitchen where he cried piteously. Despite the dramatic start, the evening passed pleasantly as we sat round our log fire and reminisced about our time in Ghana.

Surprisingly, Klump had no objection to another visitor we had. The man was about thirty years old, blind in one eye and painfully thin. He told me he was looking for work as he needed money to feed his family and he hadn't eaten for two days. We had firewood ready for chopping but, looking at the man shivering in the cold, I didn't think he would have the energy to lift the cheap axe we had bought.

'Wait here,' I said after we had stood for a moment, avoiding eye contact. I went into the kitchen and quickly made a bowl of porridge.

Adrian was surprised to see the man when he came home for lunch soon afterwards. I explained that I was feeding him up before setting him to work on the woodpile.

The man came regularly after that but I was hard pushed to find work for him. There were water restrictions at that time and we hadn't planted a garden.

I had become friends with Betsy, an American married to Tony who was English. Between us we found odd jobs for the man. For the next few weeks he shuffled back and forth between us and our guilty consciences as we gave him food and a few pula in exchange for little bits of manual labour.

A South African neighbour watched grimly and remarked that I should have sent him packing in the first place. However, he stopped coming when winter ended and I like to think that we helped him through the lean time.

Emily was excited that she would celebrate her third birthday in Mochudi. Adrian was running a week-long TAPU workshop at the teachers' centre in the museum and we had arranged to stay with George and Heather.

We left Francistown after work on Friday and five hours later were congratulating ourselves that we were nearly there when we were flagged down next to an overturned car. A man and two women were looking very shocked. They explained that the injured had already been taken to hospital but, although they themselves were not injured, they had no way of getting to their homes.

The cold night air accompanied them as we squashed up to make room. Adrian explained that he would drop us first and then take them where they needed to be. It was nearly midnight by the time we arrived at George and Heather's but it was three in the morning when Adrian got in, having taken our passengers to their villages.

We spent Saturday morning at the agricultural show on the outskirts of Mochudi. In the afternoon Poppy and the rest of the gang arrived to play with Melinda and Emily at George and Heather's 'open house'. We were delighted to hear that Heather was pregnant. She was keeping well and we all climbed Phaphane Hill on Sunday morning.

Melinda and Emily enjoyed the opportunity to see their old friends at the Day Care Centre. I was pleased to see everything running smoothly but had no regrets about my decision to do something different in Francistown. Miss Kgobe was on maternity leave so we went to see her after visiting crèche. She was nearing the end of the traditional three months period for first time mothers to stay at home. There were sticks across the gate to keep the new mother and baby inside the compound. We were told to lift up the sticks and go through the gate. Miss Kgobe was sitting on a mat on the ground nursing her baby. She was delighted to see us and called her little sister to bring me a chair. Melinda and Emily squatted on the ground and wiggled their fingers at the baby who gurgled happily.

'Would you like to hold her?' Miss Kgobe asked and they nodded enthusiastically.

'My turn!' said Emily as Melinda gently rocked the baby.

I shook my head and was surprised when Miss Kgobe took the baby and placed it carefully on Emily's lap.

'I think we should go now,' I said as Emily began to rock the baby vigorously. As we left I gave Miss Kgobe some pula according to the Botswana tradition.

Emily's birthday was on our last Saturday and was enjoyed by everyone, although Adrian nearly missed it. We were surprised to see the TAPU lorry stop outside George and Heather's house at the beginning of the party. The driver said that he had come to collect Adrian to sort out some trouble. One of the TAPU men had been drinking and fallen down the steep steps leading to the museum. At some point he had ripped someone's jacket and the owner proceeded to hit him with an iron bar. When Adrian arrived the man was lying unconscious at the foot of the steps. Two hours later Adrian returned to the party having taken the man to the hospital to have his head stitched. Despite that incident the TAPU workshop was deemed a great success especially as many of the teachers already knew Adrian from his visits to schools in his previous work with in-service teacher training in the area.

Our time in Mochudi reminded me how much I missed the very busy life I had had there. I faced the perennial problem of wanting to find some sort of job that would work around the children. A few days after our return to Francistown I called in at the Institute of Adult Education to see if there was anything suitable.

The Institute was housed in a small building with three full-time staff. They ran a variety of courses including English for correspondence students. Most of them had no electricity in their houses which made studying difficult. The Institute had recently organised for participants to study in a classroom and were looking for a teacher to help anyone who requested it. I was asked to start immediately and so, every Wednesday from 5.30 to 7.30, I sat with a class of mainly female students and gave individual advice when they had a problem. At first they were hesitant about asking but, after a few sessions, I was receiving requests for help from the hard working adult students. Later I was asked to help run weekend courses which I enjoyed.

Tiny had left and Gladys now worked for us. When Adrian was away she looked after the girls on the evenings I was working. Gladys, who had grown up children of her own, was kind and unflappable. She lived in the steward's quarter in our garden and the girls loved her. I found her very pleasant company and was disappointed when she left to supervise the building of her own house.

By the end of June, people were increasingly talking about the health of the President, Seretse Khama, who had just returned from receiving medical treatment in London for pancreatic cancer. He died on 13th July aged 59.

Botswana's first president had been revered throughout the world and loved by his own citizens. 40,000 people paid their respects to Seretse Khama as his body lay in state in Gaborone.

There were two days of mourning for his funeral. He was buried in the royal cemetery on a hill in his home town of Serowe. Gladys was one of the thousands of people who flocked to Serowe for the event.

We spent the two days pottering in the garden. Adrian also needed to do some work on our Land Rover in preparation for Aunty Doff's visit in August. Dorothy was my mother's younger sister and, like my mother, had a yearning for travel but little opportunity. We were looking forward to taking her to Zimbabwe especially as we had already had a 'trial run' with Adrian's mother.

Chapter 19

Darnaway Farm, Flight of Angels and Bulawayo

We were fortunate to have hospitable friends living near Gaborone so, after picking up Aunty Doff from the airport, we stayed the night with George and Heather.

The next day we drove north to the Tropic of Capricorn then turned east towards the Limpopo and Darnaway Farm. Theo and Verna were pleased to see us and gave my mother's sister a warm welcome.

The August temperature was ideal for game viewing and we set off in Theo's truck. I was slightly apprehensive when I saw him sling some guns in the back next to Adrian. Theo explained that he hadn't sold any cattle since the outbreak of foot and mouth eight months earlier. To make matters worse, their entire crop of maize had been eaten by warthogs.

'I don't like shooting animals,' he said, 'but my workers' crops on their lands have also failed and their families have nothing to eat'.

We slowed down when we saw impala, some were grazing the tall grass while others were nibbling bark from trees and bushes.

'They're beautiful,' said Aunty Doff as she took a photo.

'Good shot!' shouted Theo.

However he wasn't referring to the camera but to an impala. On Theo's bidding Adrian had shot it from a distance of about a hundred metres. The men jumped out of the truck and loaded it into the back.

'Thanks, Adrian'. Theo looked relieved, 'That will keep my workers in meat for several weeks.'

We were quiet as we contemplated the struggles that farmers throughout Botswana were having in this often barren land. For us, the farm was somewhere to relax after our more urban life in Francistown, but Theo's problems reminded us that the reality was very different.

Theo slowed down every now and then to check livestock and fencing and to point things out to Aunty Doff.

Verna had supper waiting for us when we got back. Afterwards we showed our slides of the fishing expedition when my parents visited in January. Unlike that trip, we slept in a comfortable guest rondaval and Aunty Doff stayed in the house. This suited us better than our previous camping experience because the nights were chilly. In addition it meant that we didn't have the uncomfortable experience of seeing search lights from the South African border police vehicles as they patrolled the banks of the River Limpopo looking for fugitives escaping from the regime in their own country.

In the morning we visited Alice Beamond, the lady from South West Africa, who had given my parents some gemstones.

She greeted Aunty Doff with 'How do you like Botswana? It's a terrible country isn't it?'

It was difficult to think of an appropriate reply without causing offence to either our hostess or our host country.

I quickly handed her the bracelet my father had made from the gem stones. She was delighted and, in return, gave us a couple of pieces of pink agate which we still have.

After lunch at Darnaway we walked to the weir which had been in full torrent at Christmas. Remembering our last visit, Melinda and Emily kept their distance in case of crocodiles.

'Look at the naartjies'. Melinda pointed to the trees in the orchard when we came back from the river.

Theo laughed. 'She's a real South African girl!' He picked a handful of tangerines and passed them round.

Aunty Doff wanted to know how Darnaway Farm got its name. Theo explained that the farm originally belonged to a Scottish Earl. He told us that he had worked the land as a tenant farmer until the opportunity arose for him to buy the farm at a price he could afford.

'It's a hard life,' said Theo, 'But it means I'm accountable to no one and that's how I like it.'

Klump greeted us boisterously on our return but, like everything on that visit, Aunty Doff took it in her stride. The girls peered into her suitcase as she unpacked the gifts she had brought from my parents as well as herself.

'It feels like Christmas!' I said as I admired the blouse from my parents.

Unsurprisingly, I no longer have the blouse. However she also brought a copy of the letters page from Woman's Own magazine which I still have. My letter was entitled Transport Home and described how Emily had taken her imaginary bus with her when we moved so that she could travel back to her old home.

In those days contributors were paid for letters which impressed Adrian who joked that my career as a journalist had begun.

Aunty Doff was welcomed by our friends who, like me, were missing contact with our families at home. When we visited Betsy, Aunty Doff was pleased, although slightly surprised, when she was immediately handed Betsy's baby. She later told me that she found the way children wandered from one family to another was very different from the way children were brought up in England, as I was to find on our return.

Joe Butali, a colleague of Adrian's who had recently returned from doing a degree in education at Edinburgh University, invited us all to his cattle post. He lived in one of the government houses at the end of our road and often dropped by to discuss things with Adrian and to see how we were when Adrian was away.

We went in our Land Rover and Joe pointed out the villages that had primary schools. After about an hour we came to an area of Mopane woodland. The tall trees were verdant, very different from the mopane scrub we had driven through at Mmatsela's cattle post in the south east of

Botswana. Joe had many more cattle and the area they grazed was several times bigger.

We stopped outside the kraal which was an enclosed area with a fence of thorn bushes. Inside the kraal was a hut and a yard where a woman was pounding grain. Some children were playing and two teenage boys looked at us with interest.

'Come!' said Joe and jumped out of the vehicle. Emily was startled when a cow mooed loudly so Joe held her hand while Melinda skipped ahead; as usual both girls were barefoot. Joe joked with the boys then spoke to the woman who pointed into the wood.

He introduced us and said that Aunty Doff was a special guest from England. He chatted to them for a while then suggested we went to find the main cattle herd further on.

We got back into the Land Rover and Joe gave Adrian directions.

'Are you all right?' I asked Aunty Doff as we bumped over a particularly large tree root.

'I'm fine,' she said with a smile as she held Emily who was in danger of being bumped off her seat.

'There are the cows!' Melinda pointed to some cattle browsing the mopane trees.

'Some of them anyway,' said Joe. 'Let's go and have a look.'

We were pleased to be out of the vehicle and the girls picked some leaves to give to the cattle but stepped back quickly when one large beast stamped its hoof and made a harrumphing sound.

'Are any of these for milking?' asked Aunty Doff.

'Not these, but we have some milking cows near the kraal.'

It wasn't long before the cattle man appeared and, after nodding at us in greeting, spoke to Joe is the local language.

'What's he saying?' asked Melinda.

'He's speaking Kalanga which is the local language, I expect he's telling Joe about the cattle,' replied Adrian.

We pottered about in the shade and looked for wildlife.

'Look at that bird going for a ride!' Melinda pointed to a brown bird with a red and yellow beak sitting on one of the cows.

'It's called an oxpecker,' said Joe as he joined us. 'It's pecking ticks off the cow.'

'Yuk!' said Melinda and screwed up her face.

'The birds don't think so and the cows are pleased to have their ticks removed.' Joe smiled. 'Shall we drive round the cattle post?'

After a while we left the woodland and drove through rough grassland.

'I see the jackal's back', said Joe as we caught sight of an animal in the distance.

'Are they dangerous?' asked Aunty Doff as she pointed her camera at the animal a little bigger than Klump.

'They are if you are a small animal,' laughed Joe. 'They eat snakes which is helpful.'

We got out of the Land Rover and stretched our legs.

Adrian asked Aunty Doff if she would like to drive and I was surprised when she said yes. She managed very well but became over confident in the woodland and we came to an abrupt stop against the trunk of a tree.

'Whoops!' I said, at which Aunty Doff started to laugh slightly hysterically. This made Adrian and I laugh too but, understandably, the girls were unable to see the funny side and Joe looked rather surprised at our reaction.

'Shall I take it from here?' asked Adrian when we had calmed down.

'I think you'd better!'

We stopped briefly at the kraal where Joe picked up two containers of fresh milk. He explained that it was better than pasteurised milk which was only necessary for cows that spent their lives in overcrowded cowsheds.

Aunty Doff nodded in agreement. 'We kept a couple of cows for their milk in Wales and that's what I had when I was growing up.'

'Ah, you are like a Motswana!' laughed Joe.

Botswana schools had a two week holiday in August and we left for Zimbabwe on Monday 9th August. We did not realise that this was National Heroes day which is currently celebrated by 26 nations, mainly countries that have previously been subject to colonial rule. Botswana does not celebrate national Heroes Day so we were unaware that our arrival in Zimbabwe coincided with the first secular national holiday in Zimbabwe since the beginning of the Independence War in 1964.

Zimbabweans had flocked to the beauty spots over the week-end so, when we arrived at Wankie Game Reserve, we found that all the chalets were fully booked.

'Is there anything else?' I asked.

The receptionist shook her head, 'Only if you camp.'

As we turned to go a man pushed past us and gave the receptionist his key. 'Family crisis,' he muttered and hurried off.

She looked at us and smiled. 'You're in luck! A cabin has just become free. It's smaller than a chalet and there's a cooking area with a braai outside…

'That's a barbecue,' I whispered to Aunty Doff.

'We'll take the cabin,' said Adrian to the receptionist.

She smiled, 'It will be available later after it's been cleaned.'

Pleased that we already knew the layout from our visit with Granny Helen, we set off to look for game. The next two days were as packed with excitement as the last time. There were fewer leaves on the trees which made game viewing easier. Aunty Doff had bought binoculars for the trip which she put to good use. We saw elephants on our walk at sunset while Adrian cooked steaks on the braai and the girls made mud pies with the children staying in the next cabin.

The public holiday was over when we arrived at the Victoria Falls Motel and we enjoyed the familiarity of having stayed there in May. The girls immediately asked to go in the pool but we wanted to show Aunty Doff the Falls so we drove to the Elephant Hills Hotel for sundowners. The hotel was on a hill with an excellent view of the Falls; on the other side of the river was the town of Livingstone in Zambia. The hotel had its own golf course but the only players that evening were a group of impala.

Everyone was up early the next morning, keen to see the Falls. Although there was less water plummeting 100m into the narrow gorge than on our previous visit, the sight was still breath-taking and we got very wet walking through the rainforest on the edge of the Falls.

We went as far as the Devil's Cataract which is the lowest of the five Falls with a drop of 60m. There was no fence and the girls kept close to us as we walked carefully, hardly able to hear ourselves speak above the roar of the water.

As we retraced our steps we saw a small plane flying low over the Falls.

'That's the way to see them!' said Adrian.

Aunty Doff looked thoughtful.

Later, when we were sitting round the motel pool Aunty Doff said she would like to pay for Adrian and I to fly over the Falls and also to have a meal together as we didn't get much time on our own.

'That's a lovely idea,' I said, 'but the flight might be wasted on me. Why don't you two do it? It's only 15 minutes and we'll come and watch you.'

After lunch we went to the airstrip and booked two seats on the eight seater plane for the following morning.

As we were leaving I suggested we went to see if there were any afternoon river trips. We were fortunate to get good seats on a cruise going up the Zambezi with a stop to explore an island along the route. Our guide told us that the island was safe because all the land mines had been recently removed.

He pointed out some small balls of vegetable ivory which comes from the seeds of one type of palm tree.

'It has many uses including for making buttons and jewellery', our guide said in answer to Adrian's question.

Emily busily gathered up as many as she could carry in her T-shirt.

The monkeys were rather aggressive and our guide told us that tourists used to give then sweets and now the monkeys expected them. As we cruised further upstream we saw a troop of baboons on the river bank and a hippo in the water.

'What a flying start to the day!' I said the next morning as the girls and I watched Adrian and Aunty Doff board the plane for the Flight of Angels.

We spent the next 15 minutes looking up as the plane flew slowly over the Falls then along the river and back over the Falls several times. Nowadays, helicopters are used which are able to hover to give tourists a closer view. However, Adrian, Aunty Doff and the other passengers were full of praise for the pilot and his ability to fly so close to the Falls.

'We saw rainbows!' said Aunty Doff

'And we flew over the Devil's Cataract'. Adrian was flushed with exhilaration.

The rest of the morning was spent at the game reserve and we saw a great variety of animals. We had taken a small tape recorder to record the children's comments on the wildlife, as well as questions from Melinda such as, 'Does the monkey know he's a monkey?' Maybe we should have passed that philosophical question to David Attenborough!

Adrian and the girls spent the afternoon at the motel pool while Aunty Doff and I visited the well-stocked tourist shops. In the evening Adrian and I had dinner at the Casino Hotel.

On our last morning we went to a traditional Matabele village. Although it had been built for tourists, the people there were Matabele who lived in similar villages and were keen to answer questions. I had an interesting conversation with a witchdoctor about pregnant women and twins.

Our last sight of the Falls was from the roof garden of the Casino Hotel where we had coffee.

By the time we were in the car Melinda was running a temperature and we drove as fast as we could to Bulawayo. We checked in to Greys Inn Hotel and asked the receptionist where we could find a doctor. She recommended a surgery that was nearby.

The doctor saw us straight away and said that Melinda might have malaria or hepatitis and she should return for tests in the morning. However, after a good night's sleep Melinda was completely better. We put it down to heat exhaustion, which was not surprising as she had been swimming hard most of the previous afternoon in the relentless sunshine.

I had not noticed the wide streets on our previous visit to Bulawayo. Then, we had been greeted by jubilant crowds who, when they saw our Botswana number plate shouted, 'Welcome to Zimbabwe' and, holding onto our car, ran alongside us as Adrian drove slowly forward. Everyone was filled with euphoria for the future for independent Zimbabwe. I found out later that the streets were wide because they had originally been built with enough room for ox-drawn vehicles to turn around.

When I was a child my mother used to receive letters with interesting stamps from her friend, Barbara, who lived in Bulawayo. It was nearly 30 years since I had seen her and her family when they visited England, although I had news of her from my godmother who was Barbara's sister-in-law. Barbara's husband had died some years previously and she had re-married a widower.

I had written to Barbara saying that I was living in Francistown with my family and received an enthusiastic reply inviting us to visit.

She met us at our hotel and suggested we went to Centenary Park. It was an extensive park with a variety of trees and flowers. In the centre was a large fountain with water shooting up before cascading back down. The highlight for the girls was a ride on a miniature steam train. Barbara invited us back to her bungalow where we met her husband, Bob. I was touched when she gave each of the girls a rag doll which kept them happy while we caught up on everyone's news.

During the next four years we had regular shopping trips to Bulawayo. There was a good choice of shops including Meikles, the department store where we sometimes treated ourselves to afternoon tea on the roof terrace. There was always a welcome from Barbara whenever we called, but I sensed a sadness about the turbulence she had lived through which resulted in several of her children leaving the country that had been their home.

The day after we arrived back in Francistown Adrian had to go to Lobatse for a three day TAPU workshop, so I was very pleased to have Aunty Doff's company. She said how lovely it was to have a complete break before starting a new job in charge of all the cooking at a school for boys with behavioural and learning difficulties. The position required her to live in, which meant leaving the house where she had brought up my cousins.

'Anyway', she said positively, 'I'm only moving 30 miles, not to another country like you'.

'But we've got our house to go back to, unlike a lot of our friends here. And,' I paused then continued, 'we may be back for good if Adrian's contract isn't renewed.'

Aunty Doff's visit to Botswana finished in Mochudi where it had begun. This time, George and Heather were away so Michael invited us to stay overnight. He planned to join Nora and Tina in England as soon as the baby was born. He was interested to hear about our experience in Zimbabwe and told us that several of the Zimbabwean teachers at his school had already returned there.

I found it a wrench saying goodbye to Aunty Doff at the airport. It would be nearly a year before Adrian was entitled to home leave and we had already been in Botswana 18 months.

However, when we arrived back in Francistown, Gladys was genuinely pleased to see us and we received a lively welcome from Klump.

Chapter 20

Handicraft Survey, Maun, Vikings and Nativity Drama

Melinda was looking forward to starting school after Christmas. In the meantime she and Emily went to a nursery school run by Chris Corker, an English friend with children of her own.

I called at the Institute of Adult Education, which was usually known as IAE, to see if there were any more weekend schools and was pleased to be offered a job collating information from a survey of local handicrafts. The aim of the survey was to look at the different handicrafts produced in the area and find out if there was any connection with handicraft production and adult education activities. The survey team were university students working alongside IAE staff.

Although it wasn't necessary for the work, I was pleased that I already had some knowledge of the villages surveyed. These included Butale and Jackalas near Joe Butale's cattle post.

Before the survey it was assumed that the only items produced in this area were baskets. However, after visiting 19 villages, plus Francistown, the research team found a great variety of handicrafts including stools, walking sticks, axes, hoes, drums, xylophones and kitchen utensils.

My role initially was data processing but then I was asked to take an editorial role and finally to write the copy for A Survey of Handicrafts in the North-East District which was printed at TAPU. This led to me writing an article for 'Botswana Notes and Records', the magazine of the Botswana Society. Later I had a similar article published in Kutlwano which means mutual understanding. Both these magazines still exist and are now produced in colour.

I was able to work flexible hours over the next ten months and, although the salary was small, it enabled us to have a few treats including having a good celebration for Melinda's sixth birthday. She invited ten friends and I organised races to help them use up some of their energy. Adrian made a magnificent climbing frame which he erected the day after her birthday.

Wolfgang asked Adrian to help run a course for teachers in Maun and also asked me to do one of the sessions. He said that the girls and I would be welcome and we could all stay with him. Wolfgang's colleague, Mr Mokwathi, was currently studying in England so Wolfgang asked Joe Butali to come in his place.

The Swedish government were giving a lot of aid to Botswana, both financially and by sending Swedes to work in key roles. Lars had recently arrived to help with teacher education and Adrian suggested he also came.

About 40 teachers from Maun and the surrounding villages signed up for the course. Local women were hired to do the cooking but teachers who had not booked also turned up. This resulted in angry complaints about the amount of food provided at the end of first day.

'What can we do?' Wolfgang looked worried as he and Adrian were faced by a delegation of teachers.

'Buy a cow!' was his immediate response.

Someone was immediately dispatched to buy a large cow which provided enough meat for everyone for the rest of the week.

After that the course ran smoothly. The aim of the course was to give advice on teaching different parts of the new curriculum. On these courses Adrian took the component parts of teaching aids that had been made at TAPU and showed the teachers how to assemble them. A favourite was making sundials which helped in explaining different aspects of the curriculum. This was particularly satisfactory as the sun was generally shining. Joe's job was to explain how the changes in the curriculum were geared to give pupils an understanding of the history, geography and government of Botswana. Lars's expertise was in different approaches to teaching and learning. His aim was to boost the self-confidence of both teachers and pupils while following the curriculum.

Letter to my parents Dec 2nd 1980

The week in Maun was a success for everyone. The teachers went home with some nice aids they had made as well as confidence. I enjoyed being able to contribute with a demonstration on how to prepare and use materials for a flannel board, followed by an afternoon helping the teachers prepare their own materials. Emily sat on my knee during some of the teaching but the second day Adrian took them swimming. Melinda swam right round the pool without touching the sides and she is learning to dive. We went again on our last Sunday. Melinda was diving with a little boy and I was sitting on the side saying 'Ready, steady, go!' when suddenly there was a splash and Emily had leapt in with no armbands! Fortunately Adrian was there to haul her out. After that she kept leaping in with Adrian catching her.

The course finished on Friday morning and the teachers were very pleased with everything they had learnt.

In the afternoon we hired a plane with Joe Butali and went game viewing over Moremi Game Reserve. Whenever he spotted an animal the pilot circled back and flew very low so we could get a really good look; we were lower than the trees on several occasions. Adrian sat up with the pilot and it was nice to see him animatedly filming everything and Melinda's excited chatter as she pointed everything out: 'Mummy, mummy look, look, it's a hartebeest! Oh mummy you've missed it!' as I retched miserably into a plastic bag while Emily slept restlessly on my lap. We saw hippo lumbering towards the water and crocodile basking on the banks, giraffes, impala, marabou storks, kudu and herds of buffalo.

On Saturday we hired three canoes from Island Safari Hotel with guides to paddle through the Okavango swamps. There was Joe, Wolfgang and his dog in one canoe, Lars and Mariette from Sweden in another and us in the third canoe. Melinda and Emily loved picking water lilies that covered the river. River, in fact, is the wrong word for the myriad streams and backwaters that make up the swamps; without a guide we would have got very lost. We canoed upstream for three hours then landed on a green bank with large trees for shade. We were thinking how isolated we were when a truck hurtled past – we were by a road! Adrian cooked steaks and we lazed on the banks for several hours so that we weren't in the canoes in the heat of the day. Even so, it was very hot and the children were glad of their sunhats. Wolfgang and Joe used large water lilies instead of sun hats! We were nearly back at Island Safari Hotel when we saw a hippo in the middle of the river. They have a habit of diving under canoes and so our guides paddled into the reeds and we waited until we could just see where the hippo was before continuing quickly, keeping well into the bank.

Instead of travelling back on Sunday we decided to spend a lazy day and return on Monday. It was good we did because our bones ached from sitting in the canoe.

When Lars realised that my training was in Teaching English as a Foreign Language he asked if I would give his son, Ole, some lessons in preparation for him starting school in January. At that time Swedish children did not start school till they were seven and English wasn't taught at that age. Over the next four years I helped a number of children and adults. One, a German agriculturist told me that, in preparation for coming to Botswana, he had studied at an English summer school but the course was too general. What he really needed was a course tailored to the language he would use in his job. This made the teaching more interesting for me and valuable for the 'students' who usually only needed a few lessons.

The next Swedish family to arrive in Francistown were Nils and Marie Viking who moved in next door to us. Nils was a town planner; both he and Marie spoke good English because they had previously worked in Newcastle. Their children, Sunniva and Ambiorn were similar ages to Melinda and Emily and they picked up the language quickly from playing with them. The children felt comfortable in both our houses and Melinda told me, 'Nils is the kindest man I know apart from Grandad'.

Christmas was a good opportunity for people to get to know each other. There was a carol concert in the park with children of different nationalities. My friends, Betsy Jones and Chris Corker, were mainly responsible for the concert but they hadn't envisaged the problems that could arise from an open air venue at night. The tableaux began well with Mary and Joseph sitting in the stable with a real donkey and a real baby. Melinda and her friend Martin came on as shepherds, while we in the audience sang 'While Shepherds Watch'. Suddenly Martin let out a loud shriek when ants began to explore his feet and up his shepherd's cloak. Mrs Corker directed them to move away and sit on a bale of straw but the donkey began to nibble the straw and Melinda toppled off. The audience all held candles and there was more drama when a small fire started. Apparently the evening was regarded a success!

Although Melinda and Emily were beginning to make friends in Francistown they were still missing their friends in Mochudi so we invited Poppi for Christmas and she fitted in very well. She was very excited about Father Christmas and woke Melinda and Emily at five o'clock on Christmas morning and they all tumbled into our room to open their presents.

In the afternoon we were invited to Betsy and family and enjoyed gathering round Betsy's piano and singing carols and favourite songs.

Our Boxing Day party was enjoyed by everyone and it was a good opportunity for families to get together. We had invited Joe and his family but he couldn't come so he sent his wife and five children plus a relation and her child. Fortunately we had extra presents on the tree so there was something for all the children. When all the guests had arrived, we organised party games and then a tug-of-war for the adults; this was a popular party activity in those days.

I had been slightly anxious about how Klump would behave but he just walked around tidying up bits of food that dropped on the ground.

We were pleased to welcome Nora, Michael and family overnight on New Year's Eve on their way back from Zambia.

By the end of the first week in January Poppi was beginning to get homesick, and Melinda was starting to be anxious about starting school. Adrian had some business in Gaborone so we decided to all go and stay in Mochudi.

On the drive back I reflected on our many different experiences over the last two years and I wondered what challenges the next two years would bring.

Chapter 21

Women's Institute, Bushman Schools and Alistair

The holidays were over and Melinda was ready to go into Standard One at John Mackenzie School. It had originally been for British ex-pat children but, by this time, there were Batswana and South African children as well Europeans and Indians. The British Government paid Melinda's school fees as part of Adrian's contract.

Adrian used to drop Melinda on his way to TAPU and I went with Emily to pick her up at one o'clock. Like parents all over the world, I found this a good opportunity to meet other parents. I became particularly friendly with Ans who was Dutch. She and her husband had sons the same ages as Melinda and Emily. Another friend was Caroline Hall whose son, Jason, started school at the same time as Melinda. Caroline ran a textile workshop that produced locally designed cloth. Over the next few years our families got to know each other well.

Ans was a member of Francistown Women's Institute, W.I, and asked if I would be interested in joining. I thought it would be a good way of meeting people so I went along. Several of the members, including the chairwoman, were originally from South Africa but had settled in Francistown. Among other aims, W.I. has a commitment to public service and each year the local branches choose a local community project to support.

'How did it go?' asked Adrian when I returned from a meeting in early January.

'We were discussing what to support this year. Distributing food to some of the poorer families in Francistown is still ongoing but they are considering what else to support.'

Adrian looked thoughtful. 'You remember that Bushman school Joe and I went to, the kids there could really do with some warm clothes.' He paused, 'The head teacher said they wanted to grow a vegetable garden but they need seeds and garden tools if they are to have enough for all the pupils.'

'That sounds really good. Life can't be easy for them now they aren't able to roam the land like they used to. I'll see what they think at the next W.I meeting.'

The next time I saw Ans was at Carolien and Jan Venema's house by the river. The water was low and Melinda and Ans' boys splashed around while Emily made mud pies at the water's edge. The Dutch doctor and his wife, Welmoed, were also there. The four of us were all members of W.I. and I asked the others what they thought of the idea of supporting the Bushman school.

'It sounds a worthwhile thing to do but I'm not sure what the other members will think. How far is it from Francistown?' asked Carolien.

'Somewhere past Nata.'

'Nata's about a two hour drive from Francistown', said Ans's husband, Aard.

'I get the impression the committee don't always know what to do with the money they raise. I was surprised when they gave presents to our children this year.' I said.

'Yes, it does seem a bit unnecessary,' agreed Caroline.

I mentioned the need of the Bushman children for warm clothing at the next W.I. meeting but nothing was resolved. There was a division of opinion between the 'old guard' and those of us who were in Botswana for only as long as our husbands' contracts lasted. As well as wanting to get things done while we could, we also needed an outlet to talk about our feelings of disempowerment.

I had been angered when a man I hardly knew introduced me to his male friend as 'Mrs TAPU.' He was taken aback when I replied that I was a woman in my own right, with my own name. When I spoke to other women in a similar position to myself, some of us decided to set up a Women's Discussion Group to talk in a relaxed way about some of the issues we encountered. I was pleased, although rather surprised, to find Spare Rib, the feminist magazine, on sale in Francistown and articles from this often provoked points for our discussions. The first meeting was held in my house when Adrian was away. One of the things that several of us had in common was that our husband's often travelled away for their work and, unless they were somewhere with a phone, we had no means of contact.

Letter to my parents

Adrian arrived back after a very demanding two week trip. It's a good job he was able to repair the vehicle as he went along as he might still be in the Kalahari! However, a faulty vehicle was only part of the problem; his driver contracted meningitis and it was touch and go whether he would live. Fortunately a Sri Lankan doctor had just been appointed to Tsabong and the driver has now recovered. Adrian had to drive the vehicle back from Tsabong himself but had to abandon it at Lobatse as the doors wouldn't open! However, on the plus side, Adrian and Martha spent a day in Gemsbok Game Park and saw all the animals except lions. He also got all his spirit duplicators delivered and met several interesting people.

At their next committee meeting the W.I decided that the chairwoman and I should investigate the Bushman school. Joe Butale was pleased when I told him and said he would take us there. Unfortunately, just after passing Nata, we had to make a long detour round a flooded river. We stopped to ask a cattle herder the way but he just shook his head.

When we finally arrived, we saw that the school was housed in a new single story building. It had two classrooms and a small office for the head teacher.

It was break time and the children were playing outside. They were shorter than the Batswana children I knew, lighter skinned and their faces were slightly oriental in appearance. Most of them were wearing torn and ragged clothes. The headmaster explained that the majority of children had to care for themselves when their parents were hunting animals for food. Sometimes they were away for several days at a time. The children had been taught by their parents how to dig for particular roots with a long stick but they soon exhausted the ones near where they lived.

'This is where we want to grow vegetables,' said the headmaster as he showed us a patch he had marked out for a vegetable plot. He went on to explain that, as the parents had no income, they couldn't buy food for their children let alone contribute to the cost of seeds for a school vegetable garden.

'Does the school receive food aid?' I asked as I remembered the sacks of cereal that Mochudi Day Care Centre received from the United Nations food programme.

'It does,' said the headmaster, 'But supplies are sometimes late to arrive here. And of course there is no food aid in the school holidays.'

'I'm sure we can supply seeds and tools for the vegetable garden as well as clothes for the children,' I said as I thought of my daughters' well stocked wardrobe which was presumably similar to those of my friends' children.

The play area went quiet when one of the teachers clapped her hands and the children stood in two lines and went to their classrooms.

Joe wanted to talk to the headmaster so the chairwoman and I sat in his car with the doors open. As we drank the cold water we had brought and ate the snacks, I realised there was no comparison with the lives of the Bushman children and my own.

Suddenly, I had a memory of Melinda and Emily stamping their feet and dancing in a cave covered with Busman paintings we had come upon in Zimbabwe's Matopos Hills and I laughed.

'What's the joke?' the chairwoman asked.

I told her about my memory but she looked puzzled so I asked her if she had been to the Matopos.

'Yes, she replied, 'it's a beautiful area, did you see Rhodes grave when you were there?'

I nodded. 'We were there just before we discovered the cave paintings.'

I remembered how, on our visit to the Matopos six months earlier, we had climbed to the top of a steep granite hill strewn with massive boulders. At the top was an imposing stone slab marking the grave of Cecil Rhodes. He was the prime minister of Cape Colony in South Africa in the late 19th century and made his fortune in gold and diamond mining as well as laying down the foundations for apartheid.

'But there aren't any Bushman paintings there.'

'No, we found them quite by chance. We decided to go down the other side of the hill and came to a large cave. All around the walls were the most incredible images of animals. Fortunately the light was good enough to take photos. One image is of two giraffe and at the bottom are two tiny hunters. Another shows several hunters in the centre of the picture running across rocky terrain.'

'I haven't heard of those caves'.

'We were lucky to stumble across them. The girls had great fun pretending to be Bushmen!'

Joe shook the headmaster's hand when they came out of his office. 'This man runs a good school despite the many challenges,' he said. 'He is grateful for your visit and says the children will really benefit from your generosity.'

'We look forward to helping,' I said.

'Thank you.' The headmaster looked at the chair woman and then at me. 'Mr Butale speaks highly of you and I'm sure we can rely on your support. We have had other whites offering to help, but then we never see them again.'

'Oh, you can rely on us.' I stopped, embarrassed that I was speaking out of turn.

'It has been interesting,' said the chairwoman stiffly. 'I will inform the committee about providing clothing and items for a vegetable garden.'

'You have travelled a long way to see us. Thank you for coming'. The headmaster bowed his head slightly and accompanied us to the car.

A few weeks later I was invited to join the W.I. committee as the member responsible for projects.

Everyone connected with the school was very pleased with our involvement, particularly our donations of tools and seeds for the vegetable garden. On my next visit I was touched by the children's enthusiasm and the hard work they were putting into the garden and their pride in their 'new' clothes.

Word of our support for the Bushman school got round Francistown and we were asked to help another school even further away. A man I had met only once, called at the house and asked if I was ready to go with him to see the other school. As I hadn't received his original message I was somewhat flustered, especially when he said we would be staying overnight so he gave me two hours to pack and make arrangements for the children.

The journey took nearly five hours. I was taken aback when we came to a halt at the end of a very bumpy track. Unlike the new building at the previous school, this was a long wooden shelter, open on three sides and precariously thatched with grass. Behind were three small rondavals. The only other buildings were a small hospital outpost and a pit latrine next to it.

Ragged children stared at us as we walked to the building. The headmaster welcomed us and introduced us to the teacher. He explained that he did not have an office, just a desk at one end of the building. He clicked his fingers and told two of the boys to bring chairs for us to sit on in the scanty shade of a thorn bush.

The headmaster told us some of the problems he encountered which were similar to the other school but made worse by the lack of basic facilities.

I told him about the school we were already supporting and said that, when I had returned recently, I was impressed with their flourishing vegetable garden.

As I spoke I felt despondent as I realised the enormity of the problems of this school compared with the other. I listened to the headmaster outlining his ideas but the heat was intense and I found it difficult to concentrate after the long and unexpected journey.

In an effort to be positive I pointed to the medical building.

'I'm glad to see you have a hospital outpost,' I said.

'Yes, the nurse comes once a month. There is always a long queue of people waiting for her on those days.'

'I'm sure, a month is a long time to wait.'

'It is a good facility. You will be comfortable there tonight.'

'Oh!' I tried not to look too surprised.

In fact, it was one of the most uncomfortable nights of my life. My bed was the examination trolley which, due to my diminutive height, I found difficult to get onto and even more difficult to get off in the morning, especially when I was in a hurry to visit the latrine.

The rest of the morning passed in a blur as I did my best to concentrate while my head felt as if it was spinning. However, I promised to tell the W.I. about the school's needs and hoped that we would be able to help.

Sadly, at the next meeting it was felt that the school was too far away and, despite their obvious needs, I reluctantly agreed.

In January we had received a telegram from George and Heather, saying that their son Alistair had been born the day before.

Melinda and Emily were excited and wanted to know when they could see the baby.

'Well,' said Adrian looking pleased with himself, 'I'll see him next week when I go to Gaborone. You can buy a present and I'll give it to him from you.'

The girls were in agonies of indecision when we went shopping the next day and unsurprisingly we ended up with several presents for Alistair.

When Adrian returned he told us that George would be running some courses for literary assistants in Mahalapye in March. Heather had asked if she and Alistair could stay with us while George was away. The girls were delighted at the prospect, even though they had hoped the baby would be a girl!

We all enjoyed their stay. By then, Alistair was six weeks and taking notice of things going on around him. In the mornings Heather had time on her own when I was working on the Handicraft Survey.

During the time they were with us Alistair had a lot of new experiences. He slept through a children's film at the Club and a performance of the Mikado as well as a Woman's Discussion Group meeting at our house.

When the girls returned from school they enjoyed playing with Alistair and liked to show him their toys. Often, Sunniva would join in until she and Melinda ran outside to play on the climbing frame.

George was pleased to be with Heather and Alistair when he stayed one weekend. He enjoyed the break from his course especially as the facilities were not very good for the number of people. We talked about asking Theo and Verna if we could camp at Darnaway Farm for the weekend when the course finished. As usual, they were pleased to see us, despite having a full house with their family staying.

Flash Forward

We remained friends with George and Heather when we all returned to England. Later, they moved to Forres on the Moray coast in North East Scotland. On one of our visits they suggested we went to a nearby castle which was intriguingly called Darnaway. Apparently, the Moray family have owned and managed estates since the sixteen century, including several in Africa. We were unable to go inside the castle but had the satisfaction of knowing that, 20 years earlier, we had stayed on a farm that had once belonged to the Moray family.

Chapter 22

Kenya, Riots, Royalty and Osgodby

Life continued to be busy, including planning our journey home. I was slightly worried that Emily wouldn't recognise anyone and was pleased when my parents sent a photograph album of all the family which she enjoyed looking at. She celebrated her fourth birthday a month before we left.

When Adrian went to work the next day Elijah approached him looking anxious.

'I have been hearing about the riots in England and I think it is too dangerous for you and your family. You will be much safer here in Botswana.'

We tuned in regularly to the news on the World Service and knew about the riots that had started in Brixton where there was a large Afro-Caribbean community. Many of them were suffering from unemployment and poor housing, resulting in a higher-than-average crime rate. The riots spread to other areas of high unemployment, particularly Toxteth in Liverpool and Moss Side in Manchester.

Adrian explained that we lived in a quiet area of England where, apart from motorcycle speeding and the occasional theft of farm animals, life was relatively crime free.

We flew from Botswana to Kenya. Apart from Adrian's brief trip to Johannesburg and our visits to Bulawayo, we had not seen a city since leaving London two and a half years earlier. When we arrived at President Kenyatta airport we felt overwhelmed by the vastness of the concourse with modern shops and announcements blaring over the tannoy. It was getting dark when we haled a taxi to take us to our hotel. The driver had his hand on the horn as we sped passed tall buildings and streets bustling with people.

The hotel was several stories high and the girls looked worried when we got into the lift and gasped when it started moving upwards.

'This is fun, isn't it?' said Adrian and they nodded uncertainly.

However, they were excited when we reached our room and wanted to unpack. I explained that we were only staying the night and had to get up early in the morning to get a train to the seaside.

We had booked to stay in a lodge at Serena Beach, 20 km north of Mombasa. Once we were passed the sprawling Nairobi suburbs the five hour journey was fascinating, especially when the railway line went along the edge of the Tsavo National Park.

Mombasa, on the Indian Ocean, was founded about 1.000 years ago by Arab traders and has remained an important port ever since. The bus from the railway station to Serena Beach ran along the coast and, having been living in a land-locked country, it was a treat to see the ocean.

'Look at that sailing boat!' cried Melinda, pointing to a dhow plying its wares along the coast.

They were a regular sight from our lodge that opened directly on to a beach of white sand. The only things between our lodge and the sea were tall palm trees providing welcome shade.

The highlight of our three night stay was a trip in a glass bottom boat. We did not have to go far from the shore to see coral and many different types of fish including star fish. There were snorkels for hire so Adrian was able to get close up to the marine wild life.

We took one of the regular flights from Mombasa to Nairobi airport to begin our next step of the journey. The nearest airport to our home was Humberside which had direct flights to Amsterdam so we decided to have a two night stopover there.

Walking by canals was relaxing but for, the girls, the highlight of our stay was a visit to Madurodam miniature village near The Hague. We had bought them some Dutch clogs and their feet clattered as they ran around.

They continued to wear their clogs when we arrived in England which convinced people in our village that this was standard footwear for children in Botswana.

The sun was shining as we flew over the North Sea and looked down on fishing boats in the estuary.

'Look at all the people,' I said in surprise as we circled the small Humberside airport.

We were quiet as an announcement came over the tannoy informing us that Her Majesty the Queen was about to fly out, having officially opened the Humber Bridge.

At the time, the bridge was the longest single-span road suspension bridge in the world. As well as being an incredible feat of engineering, it meant that north and south bound traffic no longer had a long detour to the nearest road bridge over the river.

'If you look carefully, you might see the Queen,' I said.

'The same Queen we saw in Gaborone?' asked Melinda excitedly.

'Yes.' I moved back in my seat so that Melinda could have a better view.

'There she is!' said the stewardess as she checked our seat belts.

Much to most passengers delight we got a good view of the Queen as we circled the airport.

We had booked a hire car for the duration of our stay and we crammed our luggage into the small car.

40 minutes later we arrived at our house in Osgodby.

We had let our semi-detached cottage on the main street of the village to a reliable couple but they had left after a year. Our friend Julie had arranged for a teacher she knew to move in with his partner. She told us that they had left the house and garden in a poor state but she had done her best to make it ready for us and we were most grateful.

Osgodby, with its population of 300 people including surrounding farms, felt very small after Francistown but it was good to be home. The family next door had a daughter the same age as Emily and they were pleased to see us safely back from our travels. Another family with a daughter the same age as Melinda had recently moved into the detached house the other side so we were fortunate there were playmates for the girls. We also had teacher friends in Market Rasen as well as Adrian's parents in Middle Rasen. Soon after we arrived, my parents visited from Somerset and we made plans for our stay with them later in the holiday.

I was keen to spend time in London with my brother, Nigel, as well as a couple of old friends. The girls were happy with their new friends and Adrian wanted to put the garden in order so I had no qualms about going away. The journey was easy, in those days Market Rasen had a direct train service to London.

As soon as I stepped off the train at Kings Cross I felt that I was returning to my roots. I spent my childhood first in Walton-on-Thames then Weybridge and trips to London had been a regular part of my life. From the age of 15 I would make the half hour train journey to London, often on my own, and was happy wandering around, breathing in the sights and sounds of the city. My one year teacher training was at the London Institute of Education and my first year of teaching had also been in London.

Family rumour was that Nigel lived in a squat, but in fact it was a house run by Islington Community Short Life Housing. Everyone had their own room but they often gathered together for the evening meal which they took turns to cook. People either had jobs or were studying. At the time I visited, Nigel was working as a gardener.

The day after I arrived was a public holiday for the wedding of Lady Diana Spencer to Prince Charles, the heir to the throne. Normal life in London was at a standstill so I decided to join the celebrations. Even though it was early, people were already beginning to line the streets. However, the area outside St Paul's Cathedral was not crowded when

I arrived and I got a good vantage point. People were friendly and several of us admitted we had never done anything like this before. By ten o'clock the area was crowded but I was able to see a steady stream of guests walking up the cathedral steps. Around eleven o'clock I caught a glimpse of Prince Charles arriving in his naval commander uniform. Soon afterwards there was a resounding cheer when the bride arrived in the royal coach pulled by two black horses. Her five bridesmaids were careful not to step on her long white train as they followed Diana and her father into the cathedral. The ceremony was broadcast across the world as well as to the crowds at the Cathedral, Buckingham Palace and Trafalgar Square.

I spent the next few days visiting friends and places I knew. Then I caught a train to stay with my friend Mary who lived in Manchester with her husband and three daughters. I thanked her again for the money she had raised for Mochudi Day Care Centre and she was pleased to hear that it was running well. I wanted to hear about the Manchester riots and she said that it had been a worrying time. The main riots had taken place in Moss Side so Mary's family had not been personally affected but traveling in the city was difficult. She told me that police had used riot control equipment including tear gas.

The rest of our time passed pleasantly, catching up with family and friends. We were not due to return till the beginning of October and Melinda went to the small village primary school, which was nearly opposite our house. The headmaster was happy for her to enrol, even for a short time, as every child on the register helped to keep the school open. She went with Rosemary, her new friend who lived next door, and settled in well.

We decided that letting our house had caused too much trouble so we left a key with Anne and Derek, Rosemary's parents, and they promised to keep an eye on it.

'Klump will be pleased to see us,' announced Emily when she saw our cases packed.

'I'm sure he will, but Mr Mokwathi will have taken care of him when he stayed in our house.'

Adrian's job was assured for the next two years and, although we were sorry to leave, the welcome that we got from our friends on our return made us glad to be back.

Chapter 23

Khami Ruins, Norwegian Christmas and TAPU Workshop

Mogae Mokwathi was pleased to see us back at T62 and we received a rapturous welcome from Klump.

'I hope he behaved himself,' said Adrian.

'He was good company, weren't you Klump?' Mogae smiled.

After we had unloaded our luggage and looked round the garden we sat on the veranda with Mogae while the girls rushed next door to play with Sunnava and Ambijörn.

'And how is everyone at TAPU?' asked Adrian.

'Fine. The ministry sent a German volunteer and he's working in the woodwork department.'

We caught up on all the news but it was obvious that Mogae was looking forward to returning home.

When Adrian returned from work a few days later he told me that he had been impressed with Richard Alschner, the German volunteer.

'He asked if it would be possible to buy some better tools. I'll see if any of the aid organisations would be interested in donating.'

We heard laughter as Melinda and Sunnava ran through our gate followed by Emily and Ambijörn.

'I see the girls have settled back,' he said as we heard them playing next door.

'Yes, it's good to be back. Marie told me about a new family from Norway who might be interested in English lessons.'

I called to see the family the following afternoon. Elisabeth said that her daughters, Karen Kristine, aged seven, and Amalie, aged 11, were having some problems coping with English at John McKenzie school. We arranged for them to come for an hour two afternoons a week. In fact, they picked up the language quickly and left after a few lessons. Their brother, Lasse, went to the Catholic Secondary School but he was the only ex-pat student and felt out of place so he came to me for more advanced lessons. I was surprised when Elisabeth said that she would also like lessons because her English was good but she said that she wanted to take it to a higher level.

Elisabeth and I got on very well. One day she showed me photos of Norway and I was fascinated by the views of sea and mountains.

'I will show you everything when you come to visit,' she promised.

'We've had an invitation to visit Norway!' I said to Adrian after she had gone.

Melinda and Karen Kristine became good friends and our two families decided to join forces with another Norwegian family and have a camping trip to the Khami Ruins.

We had been there the year before with David, an English friend, who worked for the town planning department. He had good maps which were useful as the ruins were hard to find. They are 120 km north-east of Francistown so we made an early start.

David had told us that Khami cities rose to prominence around the time that Great Zimbabwe was founded in the 11th century. Zimbabwe is Shona for 'venerated houses'. Apparently the largest Khami city had 9,000 residents and, like Great Zimbabwe, had trade links with people from Asia and the Far East.

The weather was unseasonably cold when we set off in three cars, later than on our previous visit. The first ruin we saw was on a small kopie with the remains of a dry stone wall strewn around. Pleased to be out of the vehicles, the seven children ran to the top of the kopie, then down to examine the rocks that had once been part of the ruined city.

Melinda asked if we were going to camp there but I said we would go further on after we had had something to drink.

Feeling refreshed, we drove slowly through semi-forested scrub, taking care to avoid boulders along the way.

After about 20 minutes we came to an open area surrounded by trees. We decided it would be a good place to camp and we put up our tents. A notice on one of the trees caught my eye so I went to investigate and was interested to see that it said Barber Shop. Fortunately no one turned up for a hair-cut while we were there; in fact we did not see anyone until we were back on the road to Francistown the next day.

The ruins here were larger than the first ones and, when we looked carefully, we could see evidence of rooms and a turret on one of the outer walls. Like the first ruins, there were piles of stones where the buildings had been.

After we had investigated, we shared a picnic lunch by a small river. There were large flat rocks by the water's edge and the river was shallow enough for the children to play in afterwards.

We spent a relaxing afternoon watching the children and exchanging news about Botswana and our own countries.

As usual when camping in the bush, we gathered wood to light a fire but this time it was to keep us warm rather than keep away lions. Even so, the rustle of creatures going about their business reminded us that we were visitors and the residents had their own concerns.

The following week Melinda celebrated her seventh birthday in our garden. She invited the children of all our friends including a Canadian family who had moved into the house opposite Betsy. Rosemary and her young daughters, Pinky and Tshoganetso who were living in the accommodation in our garden, were invited too. Tshoganetso was still a baby but enjoyed watching the children running around. The sun shone and a good time was had by all.

I continued to give English lessons which kept me up to date with EFL teaching. I had resigned from the Women's Institute but enjoyed the Women's Discussion Group.

Several Scandinavian women, including Elisabeth, joined the discussions. There was also Friedel from Germany and Monica from Zambia. A Kenyan women came to one meeting and couldn't understand why we didn't get jobs, but that was one of the reasons for the group. Two of our members were working but the rest of us weren't able to get regular work as we didn't know how long our husband's contracts would be and we felt we needed to be at home as several of them were often away for their work. Adrian said that we would manage if I was working full time but the problem was that most of the jobs that would suit me were in Gaborone. However we decided to keep our eyes open in case anything suitable came up.

In December we started to prepare for our third Christmas in Botswana. It began on 13th December when we were invited to celebrate the festival of Santa Lucia at Elisabeth's house. St. Lucia was killed by the Romans because of her religious beliefs but the event is now celebrated in Scandinavia by everyone, regardless of their beliefs.

Karen Kristine, dressed in a long white dress and wearing a crown of leaves topped with candles, represented St. Lucia. She was carrying a basket of ginger biscuits and saffron buns and she sang most sweetly. At the end of the ceremony Karen Kristine gave everyone food from her basket.

We were able to return their hospitality on Christmas Day. Elisabeth's husband's parents were staying with them and we invited the whole family to come in the morning for eggnog which was a Christmas tradition of ours. It is made from brandy, milk, egg yolks, nutmeg and caster sugar. Even without the addition of alcohol, it is a pleasant drink and the children felt very grown up when they were allowed to have some.

Poppi and Cecilia were spending Christmas with us but, as usual, they took everything in their stride when our Norwegian friends arrived.

Like the previous year, our Boxing Day party included a tug of war.

In the first two months of 1982 Adrian had several trips to Gaborone as well as running teacher's courses in some of the smaller towns.

The New Year also brought new opportunities for me. Botswana had recently revised the whole primary school curriculum and it was taking time to produce relevant books. The work I had done in Mochudi on the booklet How Our Government Works had impressed Jake Swartland who was head of Curriculum Development. In December he had asked me to update a Social Studies Kit which consisted of six 15 page booklets for teachers on the new syllabus. These had been originally produced by the international African Social Studies Programme and updated by the Social Studies panel.

At the beginning of March Adrian came home early looking very pleased.

'I had a phone call today from Jake asking if you can attend a meeting of the Social Studies panel about the Social Studies Kit that you updated.'

'Gosh! That's exciting, when's the meeting?'

'The day after next! The Government is putting pressure on the department to get the new syllabus running well. There could be an opening for you!'

I felt that our roles were temporally reversed as I waved goodbye to Adrian and the girls from the seven o'clock night train. I arrived in Gaborone 12 hours later and took a taxi to an English colleague of Adrian's for a quick breakfast and freshen up.

I made my way to the meeting feeling slightly apprehensive. As the meeting progressed I found that I had good reason to be.

The Chairman of the panel was an Education Officer based in Mochudi. He had previously known me as Adrian Rosser's wife who used to collect the post when Adrian was away and was always accompanied by the children.

Unfortunately, Jake had not told me that the Chairman had been one of the writers of the original kit, otherwise I would have been more careful in my suggestions.

At the meeting he asked if I was being paid for making the updates as he hadn't been paid for doing the original. I said that I had been commissioned on a freelance basis. The meeting adjourned soon afterwards.

I left the meeting feeling upset by the attitude of the panel who had taken their lead from the Chairman.

My train didn't leave till six o'clock so I decided to treat myself to afternoon tea on the balcony of the President Hotel. It was good to see the world go by and, by the time I was on my way to the station, I was feeling better and looking forward seeing the family the next morning.

Adrian's letter: 28th March 1982

Once again the intrepid explorer has been exploring and returned safely to the fold. This time it was to the Kalahari for a teachers' workshop at Tsabong and discussions in Ghanzi and Maun. I went with Lars, a Swede, and Joe Butali the Motswana education officer. We got a truck from CTO, the government garage, it looked like a cross between an ambulance and a four coffin hearse; fully laden it wallowed like a beached whale. Halfway to Tsabong we ran into some very soft sand and got stuck as we tried to engage the four wheel drive, but it wouldn't move. Fortunately it was not long before a passing truck stopped and towed us out. From there on whenever it looked soft we dropped it into second gear and hurtled, kamikaze like, at the soft patch and got through. When we got to Tsabong we managed to sort out the gears and a CTO maintenance team visiting Tsabong fixed the problem with the brakes (the warning light was on) but it wasn't until after they had left that we found that they had 'fixed' them by cutting the wires to the light. Still, we were going on virtually deserted 'roads' of thick sand so who needs good brakes!

At the end of the course Lars, Joe and myself set off for the north. We drove for two hours and found a camping spot just past Mabasehube game reserve. We collected firewood, four fairly large trees and a few smaller ones, arranged the truck for sleeping in and settled down to a meal of goat washed down by sufficient beer. For seconds we had more goat with vodka. The stars seemed to be rotating a little faster in the heavens than usual as I settled myself on top of the truck to sleep.

The next morning we set off on the next 500 km part of the journey to Ghanzi. We saw a few animals, hartebeests, steenbok, a springbok that refused to spring, gemsbok (that fabled unicorn when seen from one side) and lots of ostriches with young. We drove alongside one female sprinting at 50 km/hr and she didn't seem to be going at full speed.

About 100 km south of Ghanzi we smelt petrol and found to our dismay that the 200 litre drum had bounced around so much that it had split so we hurriedly syphoned what we could into the fuel tanks, patched the split with epoxy putty, cleaned out the back of the truck by spreading dust dry sand on the spill and sweeping it, then repacking and getting to Ghanzi at about 7.30 pm. On the road we had seen only three vehicles going the other way in the whole 500 km. After we had finished our work in Ghanzi and the CTO had fixed the brakes properly (the trouble was that the brake shoes had become detached from their springs and were rolling around loose in the drum), we set off for Maun.

The road is very bumpy and the vibration caused the battery to break its mountings and fall on the engine and spray acid everywhere. (It certainly cleaned the engine). The servo system split so the brakes were even less effective. When the body-work had rubbed sufficiently on the brake pipe to the front brakes to wear it through we didn't have any brakes left at all. That made the last 100 km in the dark through the rain along a cow-infested road quite interesting. We stopped at Lake Ngami and drove down the shore line to be greeted by the sight of thousands of pelicans and marabou storks settled down for the night. Incredible.

We arrived at Maun at about 9.30 and, as Mariette, Lars' friend, wasn't in, we sorted out the truck once again to sleep in. We brewed some milo to settle the beer and gin we had drunk at supper and, just as we got in our sleeping bags, Mariette arrived home, quite surprised to see us. I went back to bed quite soon only to be woken an hour later by heavy rain on my head. Refreshed by this sleep we stayed up chattering (non-too coherently I suspect) until about 5.30 am on Sunday morning so we were able to rest.

On Monday we took the virtually dead truck to CTO and arranged another truck to take us back to Francistown. We got back safe and sound and a little dusty as we had to travel in the back of the truck. And so back to the more normal work I'm here to do.

PS: Melinda is competing in the school swimming gala on Saturday by dint of her speed. Emily is also competing and can swim 20 m without stopping but with much changing of style and doing a large amount underwater.

PPS: Heather is in the running for a job as a Curriculum Development Officer for Social Studies.

Chapter 24

Safaris to Sua Pan, Lake Kyle and Umtali

Letter to my parents April 14th 1982

I hope you had a nice Easter. I had hepatitis but am okay now. It completely knocked me out for nearly a week.

Despite being weak, I thoroughly enjoyed the night we spent at Sua Pan on Easter Saturday. Thank goodness we never made it with you, there is nothing there, just a sparkling white pan and a few tufts of grass. We went with Caroline and Jason and also the Russell family. Our Canadian friends and another English family were already there. Later some bikers arrived, four men and a woman on motorbikes. They were lovely people and gave the kids rides. Everyone was surprised when I joined the queue waiting for a thrilling experience but I thoroughly enjoyed it!

Melinda beat the boys in the swimming gala and Emily, being the smallest, stole the show!

Thank you for my lovely earrings which I'm afraid I opened before my birthday!

Love, Heather

Letter to my Parents May 1982

We had been dreaming of this trip to the mountains of Zimbabwe throughout the months of gazing at dried-up vegetation in this waterless land of ours. As it happened, we packed the car in a torrential downpour and wallowed the 100 km along the mainly dirt road to the border. When we reached Fort Victoria people gazed in envy at our mud-stricken vehicle because they, too, had been suffering from drought.

Lake Kyle is the most fascinating man-made lake I have seen. It is a myriad of little creeks and whichever direction you walk you can see the lake. The camp site was beautiful and, to Melinda's delight, we were invited to join some families from Fort Victoria who were caravanning there for the weekend. After we had cooked our meat Adrian was happy to take Emily to bed but Melinda and I stayed for a few games of consequences which everyone took very seriously. Rain stopped play but the next morning the sun shone brilliantly and the girls played in the water which had waves like the sea while Adrian kept a watchful eye for hippos.

The Zimbabwe ruins are on the other side of the lake but, by the time we were there, the mist had come down and we were enveloped in cloud so our visit was disappointing. We saw enough to decide that we would like to go again, the ruins are far more extensive than the Khami ruins.

The highlight of our stay at Lake Kyle was on our third day when Melinda and Adrian hired horses and went tracking with a game scout. Melinda was leading when they came across a rhinoceros! They also saw giraffe, wildebeest and a variety of buck. We went into Fort Victoria for lunch and it was like a trip back to the 50s! One advantage of that was that we were able to buy old-fashioned plastic macs!

The next day we followed the hills north to Umtali (Mutari) where they turned into mountains. The road was windy, the weather drizzly, Emily felt sick and Melinda had a headache but the views were breath taking, real mountains at last! But instead of Alpine chalets or stone cottages there were round mud huts thatched with grass, life must be hard for the people who live there. The national park is called Inyanga. We drove higher and higher until we were at the far end of the Mozambique border. As it was drizzling we by-passed the camp site and made for the Troutbeck Inn, a luxury hotel overlooking a small lake stocked with trout and with pine forests on the mountain slopes. Small waterfalls tricked down to the lake and some whites had even built Swiss style chalets on the mountainside. All the rooms faced this view and we enjoyed stepping out of our window and onto the terraced lawns. A brisk walk round the lake gave us an appetite for breakfast then the girls had a quick dip in the icy water of the swimming pool followed by a hot bath. Later we took a dingy out on the lake then Melinda and Emily went riding for an hour. When they came trotting back across the lawns the groom greeted me with 'They are wonderful!' That made my day! After lunch we went to World's View and looked at mountains and valleys before making our way to the camp site.

As soon as we had pitched our tent among the pines an 18 year old English boy nosed us out like a frolicsome puppy. He told us his name was Sam and he had arrived in Zimbabwe on a one way-ticket. He was receiving board and lodging in return for teaching at St Augustine's Catholic Mission school at Penhalonga. This happened to be the school that our friend, Tino, had been to and returned there to teach after he left Durham University where he and Adrian had met. We were eager for news of him so Sam suggested we went to the school with him. He was camping with three other lads, all on one-way tickets, and one of them about to be deported because he hadn't been able to organise a job. The boys had no tent and very little food. We spent the two evenings with them sitting around a huge log fire, cooking toast and discussing the invasion of the Falkland Islands.

One of the things we especially liked about Inyanga was being able to go for long walks; previously we had either been in game parks where you can't get out of the car or it's been too hot anyway. The only thing we did not like was coming across the old Arab and Portuguese slave route crossing East Africa to the Indian Ocean. The scenery was beautiful and the sun was shining but we shivered as we imagined the slaves in shackles on their way to an unknown destination. We pulled ourselves together when we realised that the girls were giving us funny looks.

In the afternoon we all went pony trekking which was wonderful although I'm still saddle sore. I enjoyed it so much that I'm going to take riding lessons in preparation for the next trip.

The next morning we were awakened with a cup of tea from the lads. We had promised we would to give them a lift to Penhalonga. Our car had seemed full before but with addition of four young men plus kit we looked like and African bus. We now have a Datsun King Cab with a canopy over the pick-up part and two inward facing seats behind the front seats. Melinda was in her element riding in the back with two of the boys, we managed to squeeze the other two into the child-size seats in the cab and Emily sat on my knee.

We took the scenic route and spent some time at a waterfall which is higher than Victoria Falls, less water of course but spectacular nevertheless.

Penhalonga exists because of the goldmine. Fifty years ago the Fathers arrived and were given an unwanted hill above the mine. Now, the hill is home to the mission, a clinic, a large church and one of the best secondary schools in Zimbabwe.

The Fathers, an English order, were most hospitable, they gave us a guest house and pressed us to stay for two nights. Melinda and Emily were in their element because they met Daisy (8) and Orlando (6) the delightful children of an equally delightful and amazing English couple who had bought one-way tickets to Zimbabwe immediately after Independence. They have been at the school two years and they love independent Zimbabwe; many of their friends are Comrades (former guerrillas). Daisy and Orlando attend the local school and are apparently doing well. Their mother used to be dress designer and is now running an Oxfam feeding programme.

We had a day trip from Penhalonga to the Vumba Mountains. Vumba means mist and they were, in fact, enveloped in mist most of the day but we were able to glimpse the occasional breath-taking view into

Mozambique. There was no petrol in Umtali but we were able to fill up at a private pump as long as we bought lunch at the hotel. It was called Leopards Rock Hotel and was just like visiting an English stately home. We thoroughly enjoyed our five course lunch. We looked at the camp site where we had planned to stay, it was in the Botanical Gardens and there were masses of azaleas as well as tropical plants. It was lovely but by three o'clock the mist had come down and we were very pleased to return to the mission.

The next day was a 600 km drive to Bulawayo, we were pleased that we had a selection of story tapes to listen to. We arrived at five o'clock, booked in at Greys Inn then walked to the city park just round the corner where Melinda and Emily had their last romp barefoot on real grass before returning to Botswana.

The last morning of our holiday we went round the second-hand shops that were full of items from whites who were leaving. Among other things, we bought a typist's chair for $15 and lots of books including blue leather bound Collins Classics which are now out of print.

Melinda and Emily wanted to buy a guinea pig to replace the one that we assumed Klump had eaten when we went away at New Year but we refused. This was fortunate because the day after our return to T62 the gardener in the house next-door-but-one found a little furry animal which, on closer inspection, proved to be our guinea pig! We should have guessed that Klump didn't have the wits to eat him although he had pulled his cage down!

It was lovely to have such a super trip before I start my job with Curriculum Development next month.

Flash Forward

A few years later I was in Market Rasen library when I came across 'A Family Outing in Africa' by Charles and Janie Hampton. It described their journey back to England via Zaire, Rwanda and Kenya. I was so interested to read about the family we had met in Zimbabwe that I bought my own copy of the book.

We moved to Oxford in 2002. The following year Melinda and I attended an event at the Oxford Literary Festival where Janie was talking about her biography of Joyce Grenfell. Her husband and grown up children were there and were most surprised when we turned up with her Family Outing in Africa to sign. Daisy and Orlando remembered Melinda and the three of them enjoyed having a brief reminisce about their experiences growing up in Africa.

Chapter 25

Curriculum Development, Friendship and a Gift

I began work as the Curriculum Development Officer for Social Studies at the beginning of July. Apart from TAPU, the rest of the department was based in Gaborone but I was allowed to work from TAPU.

There was no formal interview because the Botswana government was putting pressure on Jake Swartland, head of department, to get books into schools. He was pleased with the work I had already done and knew he could rely on me.

My job was to liaise with teachers about problems with the syllabus and then to provide relevant text books. In practical terms this meant writing the books myself. I was particularly excited about the job because it was what I had been prepared for when I did my post-grad teacher training in London at the Department of Education in Tropical Areas, as it was quaintly called in the sixties and seventies.

On my first day I visited a primary school in Francistown to find out what problems the teachers had with the new syllabus. I was well received and it was an interesting and useful day.

The next day Hendrix, the TAPU driver, took me in the Government truck to Gaborone. We arrived in the afternoon and, after checking in at the President Hotel, I went to see Jake, who had been promoted to Deputy Permanent Secretary, and he briefed me on my role.

I felt a sense of freedom wandering round Gaborone. It had grown a lot in two years and there was far more going on. In the evening I went to a lecture at the Botswana Society.

I had been invited to the American Women's Society dinner due to my connection with them over the Day Care Centre and was pleased that I was able to attend the following evening. A large group of Americans had recently arrived, several of them the wives of people in the education sector.

During the week there was a course for teachers in Lobatse on the new syllabuses, with Social Studies scheduled for last day. Nora and Michael had been transferred to Lobatse so I had lunch with them. Gill had also moved from Mochudi so I spent the afternoon in her apartment planning what I would say to 20 teachers the following day. In the evening we took part in a darts match which I thoroughly enjoyed.

Friday was the first time I really had to show my paces as the Curriculum Development Officer. I sat with the panel of teachers and two Education Officers but the Chairman was unable to attend. We had to explain to the teachers why there was a new syllabus but no books. It was very helpful for me in finding out what to start on. We finished with a practical session and I got the teachers to make puppets from cloth and toilet rolls, then each group acted a play from a different topic from the syllabus. Most of them had never made puppets before but the results were excellent. The plays were also interesting and very amusing.

Adrian and the girls were at the Friday film at the Club when I arrived home which gave me time to unwind after being away. We were all very pleased to see each other and the girls were delighted with their presents from Gaborone.

At the beginning of July the secretary of the Social Studies panel asked me to attend the next meeting. I phoned the Chairman at his office in Mochudi to ask what was on the agenda but he said it had been cancelled.

'But why wasn't I informed? I've made all my arrangements to come', I said in disbelief.

After a difficult few minutes I realised that he had not been told of my appointment so I apologised and suggested we met to discuss the syllabus. He said he would get in touch with Jake to find out what areas I would be doing and what the panel would be doing and he didn't seem to agree when I said that I thought we should be working together.

The same thing happened again at the end of July. This time I had already arrived in Gaborone.

Jake was surprised to see me when I called at his office but was courteous as always. He said that he did not know why the Chairman had cancelled the meeting.

'I know you are busy, but I wonder if you could define my role,' I said politely.

He explained that my job was to co-ordinate the work of the Social Studies panel, sit on the Co-ordinating panel and work out policy. I think we both knew that this wasn't going to be easy with me based in Francistown.

'The most important thing,' said Jake, 'is to get materials into schools which will help teachers with the new syllabus.'

I thanked him and called in on my new colleagues at Curriculum Development. They were friendly and we chatted for a while about what everyone was doing.

I spent the night at the President Hotel and was pleased that I was staying the following night in Mochudi.

As there was no meeting, the next day was an anti-climax. I went to the Botswana Book Centre and was browsing through some magazines when the manager saw me.

'How is Francistown?' he asked.

I was touched that he remembered me. 'It's good but there isn't a bookshop.'

'Have you seen this new paper? It has only just been launched.'

He handed me a copy of the Botswana Guardian.

I looked at the front page. 'This looks far more detailed than the Government newspaper.'

'It is. They are independent and have good reporters. But most of the news is about Gaborone.'

'Maybe I should send in something about Francistown', I laughed.

'I look forward to seeing your name in the paper!' he smiled then turned away as a customer came to speak to him.

Hendrix came from Mochudi and was pleased that we were staying the night there. The town had grown since my last visit and it didn't feel the same now that several friends had moved away. However, Mmatsela and Hugh were pleased to see me and it was good to be reminded of the reality of life for the majority of people in Botswana. They were waiting to be connected to mains electricity and it was pleasant chatting outside by the light of paraffin lamps.

'Has the drought affected you?' I asked.

'It's very bad', said Hugh. 'There has been very little water in Mochudi for over a month.'

Mmatsela nodded. 'My cousin took her bucket to six empty standpipes until coming here and getting it from our rain barrel'.

'We can only use the toilet for emergencies,' added Hugh, 'so we mainly use the outside loo.'

At the end of the evening I walked under the stars to the pit latrine at the bottom of the garden then back to the house for a comfortable night's sleep.

When Hendrix wasn't available to drive me to meetings I took the night sleeper. After a busy day in Gaborone or Lobatse I enjoyed sitting in the dining car, people watching and occasionally chatting to fellow passengers. However I did not welcome the suggestions I had a couple of times from men who wanted to accompany me back to my compartment for the night. I left the dining car more quickly than I had intended, this was a downside to the job that I hadn't anticipated!

Life continued to be busy. I enjoyed going into schools and helping teachers with the new curriculum. They suggested the type of books that would be helpful and we ran courses at TAPU which ended up with us producing books for both teachers and pupils.

School holidays and afternoons continued to be a problem and I was fortunate I had several good friends to help out. Sadly, several of them were on two year contracts which were due to finish. In August we said goodbye to our

Canadian friends. Emily and their daughter were special friends and Emily cried all the way home; she slept for 12 hours but woke up crying. Fortunately, Adrian had arranged to take the girls camping in Maun with Inez, Tony and their two boys as it was a mid-term holiday. Emily cheered up when she put her little suitcase in the car.

I decided to fast while they were away which gave Rosemary a break from preparing meals. It was good to know that she and her children were on the premises. I felt faint on the first day but had enough energy to cycle to TAPU on the brightly coloured bicycle I had bought from an American volunteer. Klump had a tendency to follow so I asked Rosemary to close the gate quickly behind me. However, I was later followed by some boys shouting 'Lift!' which made me wobble on the uneven surface.

I was pleased to see Adrian and the girls when they tumbled out of the car although it was quite a shock after my four day fast, especially as the girls smelt as if they hadn't washed during that time!

A few days later I had a surprise visit from Sister Dagwe, the midwife from the hospital, who I hadn't seen for nearly two years. During that time she had adopted a Bushman family and she brought them to meet me. As well as wanting clothes for them she invited me to her cattle post where some Bushman lived.

'I know you are a writer,' she said, 'And you might like to write about the Basarawa. I think you will want to tell the people in England about Botswana.'

I said that I could give her some clothes within the next few days and I would be pleased to take photos at her cattle post as well as the school at Manxotae. Later I sent the article to the Sunday Times colour supplement, but perhaps I was aiming too high because it was not published.

There continued to be problems when I met the Social Studies panel but I had an interesting meeting with lecturers from Botswana's teacher training colleges who stressed the importance of teaching about the Bushman in a constructive way. One lecturer in particular felt very strongly about the inferior status of the Bushmen in Tswana society.

In early October our friends, Jo and David Ben-Tovim, suggested we went to Bulawayo for the weekend. They had a baby and a four year old daughter. We planned to drive but the situation in Zimbabwe had changed and the road to Bulawayo was considered unsafe. Unfortunately the tribal problems between the Ndebele people in the area and the majority Shona in the rest of the country had re-surfaced. The latest skirmish had flowed over to Botswana and we heard that there were bandits on the road so we went by train. Jo and David were both doctors in Francistown and sometimes sent patients for treatment in Bulawayo which still had an excellent hospital.

I looked out of the window at the dry landscape. Like Botswana, this part of Zimbabwe was experiencing drought. We heard that people trekked to distant boreholes only to be told that that they were reserved for people of that area only.

We had booked adjoining chalets at one of the camp sites near the town centre and, although the grass was dried up, there was water available and a small swimming pool. Despite the problems, the shops were well stocked and, as well as relaxing by the pool, we bought things that were unavailable in Francistown.

Melinda was looking forward to her birthday party later in the month. The Vikings returned from Sweden and the Corkers from England and we said that Melinda could invite as many children as she liked to her party.

It had rained the week before so there was grass in our garden and leaves on the trees and shrubs. Melinda invited 20 children, including several boys. Instead of the usual party tea we had a barbecue which our friends enjoyed and the party continued into the evening.

Soon after Melinda's party Adrian took himself off to the Limpopo to stay with Theo and Verna for three days as he was getting fed up with all the administration at TAPU and felt he wanted to do some 'real work'.

I felt exhausted but put it down to being busy. However, I began to feel nauseous and when it didn't improve I went to see Dries, our gynaecologist friend, at the hospital.

Adrian was ecstatic when I told him we would be having an addition to our family and so were the girls. I knew from experience that once, I got over my sickness, I would be excited too but the next few months weren't easy.

I was confident with the pre-natal care and assumed that the baby would be born in Francistown. Things became complicated when we heard that the British Government had passed a new law which made it a risky option in the future for the children of those born outside the UK. If our children followed in our footsteps and chose to live overseas we did not want their children, who would be our grandchildren, to be denied British citizenship.

The baby was due in mid-July and we decided that I would travel back at the beginning of June and Adrian, Melinda and Emily would arrive the week before the due date. I had no problem about going to the hospital in Lincoln where Emily was born and knew I could rely on friends in Osgodby and Market Rasen.

The four of us spent a lot of time arguing amicably about what to call the baby. Adrian said that, regardless of whether it was a boy or a girl, it would be called Neo which is Setswana for Gift. We all agreed, then came the difficult task of choosing the first name. Ignoring Adrian's suggestion that it would be Rasputin Zacharias if it was a boy, we decided on something safe. However, the girls really wanted a sister; Emily suggested Ballerina and we finally decided on Alyrene Neo.

In the meantime I had a job to do and, once I had got over the worst of the sickness, I was able to attend meetings again in Gaborone and Lobatse.

An American joined the panel but rarely attended meetings. When I asked him how teachers in Gaborone were finding the new curriculum he didn't seem to know.

He wasn't present at a particularly interesting two day workshop for text book writers organised by the publisher Macmillan. Bessie Head, a coloured South African who had made her home in Serowe, ran several of the workshops. I had read most of her books and found them enjoyable as well as being an excellent insight into rural life in Botswana. We met several times after that and I was sad when I heard that she died just before her fiftieth birthday the year after we left Botswana.

I continued to work with teachers on booklets that were printed at TAPU. Elijah came with me to a village to take photos for one of the books. We spoke to one of the elders who wanted to pass on his knowledge but he was obviously unwell, in fact neither of us had ever seen anyone looking so thin.

When Adrian was away I would sometimes work in the office which he shared with his typist, Melody. We got on very well and I realised how difficult her life was compared to mine. She was a single parent of young children and she was worried about her mother who lived in the part of Zimbabwe where the troubles were.

A woman I felt particularly sorry for was Cecilia who was also pregnant. She was 34 and already had four children. She was very upset about her pregnancy especially as she had recently been put in charge of the new printing machine. This gave her the highest status out of the six people in the print room. Now she was unable to cope with standing up all day and had asked Adrian to give her a sitting down job. A man was put in charge of 'her' machine.

January 1983 saw changes in the way people all over the world would communicate. Adrian bought a small computer and enjoyed feeding in programmes for the girls. He was also busy learning to use all the new printing equipment at TAPU.

My energy had begun to return and this was a time for new beginnings. The last time I had seen Jake Swartland he had reiterated that the most important part of my job at this stage was to get on with writing supplementary readers.

Curriculum Development was now run by an educationalist who was originally from South Africa. Unsurprising, he had difficulty in understanding why I was allowed to work from Francistown when the rest of the panel were based in Gaborone. Adrian told me he seemed to be particularly friendly with the American on the Social Studies panel.

Fortunately, my relationship with the Chairman of the panel had improved. We had a good meeting in Lobatse in March. Two editors from Macmillan Publishing had been invited to discuss the publication of an atlas for Botswana and they took us all out for lunch at the Cumberland Hotel.

I was entitled to maternity leave as long as my boss agreed. Despite the problems, I still wanted to take what I was entitled to. I had lost my job at the Teacher Training College in Nigeria after Melinda was born and it seemed as if history was about to repeat itself.

It was several months later that I found out the real reason my contract hadn't been renewed and by then I was very happy with my life and the new opportunities that came with it.

Flash Forward

Twenty years after our return to England, Adrian I were employed on a freelance basis by Macmillan Education to write text books for schools throughout English-speaking Africa. This included visits to Uganda and South Sudan where we met local teachers to discuss books for the Social Studies and Science syllabuses.

Chapter 26

Cape Verde, Early and Late Arrivals, and Wolfgang

Autumnal weather began to set in during May with winds whipping leaves off the trees. Adrian and I continued to be busy and none of us were looking forward to me leaving.

Early in the morning of May 13th I heard a scream just outside the house. We rushed out and found Melinda in the car port staring at Klump who must have died in the night. She was distraught but I was secretly relieved as I had been worried about how he would react to the baby.

My departure at the beginning of June was a mixture of sadness at leaving and anticipation for the reason. I dozed in and out of sleep on the South African Airways flight but woke up in surprise when I heard an announcement saying that we were stopping at the Cape Verde Islands.

I asked one of the stewards if there was a problem.

He shook his head. 'We always stop at Cape Verde for re-fuelling.'

'We didn't stop when I came from London to Johannesburg,' I said.

'Sometimes we don't need to re-fuel at night.' The steward looked slightly uncomfortable.

I glanced out of the window as we flew towards a small airport amid a sea of sand.

'We don't stop long; you will be able to get some fresh air,' the steward said encouragingly.

The air was stiflingly hot as I walked slowly round the airport and tried to shield myself from the sun's glare. For once, my curiosity at experiencing a new place had deserted me.

'It's not time yet, just stay where you are,' I muttered under my breath as I felt a fluttering inside me.

Once we were back on the plane I began to relax, although I was still puzzled why it had been necessary to re-fuel on one flight but not the other.

Later, Adrian's brother, who had worked for various airlines, explained that South African Airways was banned from flying over most countries in Africa but at night they often took a risk and flew very high over West Africa which meant that they were able to go the whole way without having to re-fuel.

I was relieved to see David Ben-Tovim when I arrived at Heathrow. The family now lived in Richmond and it was an easy drive from the airport. It was good to see them again and they wanted to know the latest news from Francistown. After an enjoyable two night stay I felt refreshed and ready to go back to Lincolnshire.

Katy Hiley was waiting for me at Market Rasen station. When we first met, Adrian and her husband Paul were both working at De Aston School in Market Rasen. The family had returned from Zambia just before we came back from Nigeria and, with so much in common including each having two daughters of similar ages we had immediately become friends.

'It's lovely to see you!' I said as I got off the train. 'And you must be Emma!' I smiled at the toddler staring up at me.

'I'll take your case,' said Katy after an emotional greeting. 'You don't mind walking do you?'

'Not at all, I've always envied you living just round the corner from the station.'

Three minutes later we were in her house.

'Anya and Sarah are at school but they'll be home soon'.

The family had generously said that I was welcome to stay with them until Adrian and the girls arrived.

It felt comfortable to be back on familiar ground and I enjoyed having the girls around. For the first time in several years I was at liberty to relax into a slower pace of life, unlike Katy and Paul. As well as their jobs, they were starting up a New Life Church and appreciated the time I spent with their children when they were busy.

I took the train to see my parents in Somerset and stayed overnight with my school friend, Anne and her husband, on my way back.

My friend, Mary, came from Manchester to see me and we spent a pleasant weekend at home in Osgodby. She was pleased to hear that the Day Care Centre in Mochudi was still running well.

George, Heather and Alistair visited me the weekend before Adrian and the girls were due to arrive. It was good to see them, especially as Heather was seven months pregnant, and we laughed that her bump was nearly as big as mine. The weather was lovely and on Sunday morning we walked to a gymkhana in the next village which was just over a mile away. I enjoyed meeting people I knew, although they found it hard to believe that I had travelled from Africa on my own in my condition. The walk back was slightly uphill and I was feeling breathless by the time I arrived.

After a light lunch George and Heather got ready to drive home to Oakham. They came downstairs to find Alistair staring at me while I clutched the table, breathing heavily. There was no hiding the truth, my labour pains had started!

After a quick conference it was decided that George would drive Heather and I to Market Rasen and then go home with Alistair.

I described my symptoms when I phoned the hospital and they said I should phone again nearer the time. There was almost a party atmosphere at Katy and Paul's house that afternoon and evening. Anya and Sarah kept offering me food and Emma jumped up and down knowing something exciting was going on. Hearing that women in labour suffered from cold feet, Paul leant me a pair of his socks.

At 10 o'clock I decided it was time to go, so Katy phoned the hospital to say we were on our way. There was hardly any traffic and we arrived at Lincoln hospital at 10.30.

A nurse was waiting for us as we drove up to the door and she solicitously took Heather's arm when she got out of the car. The nurse was taken aback when Heather said she wasn't the patient and pointed to me as I lumbered from the car. I was immediately put on a trolley with Heather walking anxiously beside.

Emily had been born in Lincoln hospital six years earlier and I had a comfortable feeling of familiarity as I was wheeled to the delivery ward.

All these years later, my only regret is that I never properly thanked the midwife, not just for her skilled delivery, but for her quick understanding of our situation. Alyrene was born at 3.00 am on Monday 11th July 1983. After the midwife had made sure Alyrene and I were comfortable and given Heather and myself a much needed cup of tea she left us alone for nearly two hours.

Feeling a sense of euphoria after the worries of the last few months I relaxed while Heather and I chatted and dozed. It was getting light when the midwife returned.

'I didn't want to turn you out in the middle of the night,' she said and handed Heather a pass which entitled her to have breakfast in the nurses' canteen.

When I phoned Heather a couple of days later, she told me it was an experience she would never forget. She said that she left the hospital as the sun was rising and walked past Lincoln Cathedral to the joyful sound of bells.

There were three other women in the light and airy ward. They smiled and waved to me when the breakfast trolley arrived and I wondered if I looked as exhausted as they did.

With Alyrene in a cot at my side I drifted off to sleep but was awoken later in the morning by a nurse telling me I had a visitor.

'Wolfgang!' I cried in amazement. 'How did you know I was here?'

'I knew you were having a baby so I came to the hospital.'

'Yes but,' I stopped not having the heart to tell him that she was a week early.

Wolfgang looked uneasily around the room, suddenly aware of where he was.

'Anyway, it's wonderful to see you, especially as Adrian and the girls aren't here,' I said.

'Oh, I thought they would be with you.'

'They arrive tomorrow. Where are you staying?'

'In the youth hostel, I'm cycling round England.'

He told me about his trip so far and, much to the interest and bewilderment of the other patients, I updated him on the latest news from Botswana.

After checking exactly where we lived, Wolfgang said he would see us all the next day.

In the afternoon Katy brought Adrian's parents to see their new granddaughter. His father, who was a man of few words, handed me a large box of Black Magic chocolates. 'The usual,' he said in his gruff way.

'Your Osgodby friends send their love,' said Katy. 'Angela says she'll pick you up tomorrow'.

'I hope we are all home before Wolfgang arrives,' I said and told them about his visit.

'He's a good friend,' I added, 'He and Adrian often worked together but he was always interested in the work I was doing and he was kind to the girls.'

The following afternoon I was sitting in Angela's car holding Alyrene in my arms. She drove very carefully and I relaxed in the knowledge that it wouldn't be long before our family of five would be together.

'Your German friend arrived just before I left,' said Angela. 'Anne took charge of him.'

Anne, my next door neighbour, was an attractive woman in her middle thirties.

'Wolfgang must have enjoyed that,' I said.

Angela has a great sense of humour and a laugh to match.

'I think he was terrified. Anne suggested she took him upstairs to see her paintings!'

190

Not wanting to wake Alyrene, I stifled my laughter and she gave a contented sigh as I rocked her.

Angela drove slowly along Main Street and stopped at my house, which was opposite hers, then helped me out of the car.

'Hello!' I felt slightly confused to see Anne and Wolfgang standing together.

Anne hurried forward. 'She's beautiful,' she said as she looked down at Alyrene.

I was about to reply when I heard the phone ringing in my house. I handed my key to Angela, followed her slowly inside and picked up the phone.

'It's Katy. Adrian's on his way, he thought you would be at our house. At the speed he was driving he'll be with you any minute!'

'That's lovely, I hadn't expected him so soon.'

I sank onto the settee and vaguely wondered if the plane had been early but Melinda told me later that she never knew that cars could go so fast!

As it happened, the first person Adrian saw when he screeched to a halt outside our house was Wolfgang.

The next two days passed in a blur, it was enough for me to know that we were all together again.

My parents came and stayed for a week.

'Helen and Ernest are lucky they can see the girls often,' my mother said wistfully as they were leaving.

'Only for two more weeks. Anyway, we'll be home next summer.'

Jill, Dave and their children came for two nights. We reminisced about our time together in Nigeria and how, when Melinda was six months old, we had visited Jill in hospital just after Jemima was born.

Jill was sympathetic when I told her how I had lost my job but we both agreed it was for the best.

'What will you do when you go back?' she asked.

I told her that I had started writing a novel and there would also be opportunities for more free-lance writing.

By the time we got on our plane back to Botswana we were all exhausted. The flight was full and I noticed there were several passengers travelling with babies. Eating supper with a baby on my lap wasn't easy and when one of the stewards asked if I would like him to look after the baby I gratefully handed her over. I looked up later to see several charmingly camp stewards parading with babies in their arms each claiming that their baby was the most beautiful!

Alyrene was gently handed back to me and we both slept soundly for the rest of the flight.

Chapter 27

Espionage, Celebrations, Arabella and Refugees

Apart from the uncomfortable feeling of surveillance at Johannesburg airport when we changed planes, everything went well and it was good to be back in Botswana.

We stayed overnight in Gaborone with Adrian's American colleague and his wife. I was touched by their welcome and their concern for my welfare.

The next time Adrian visited them they mentioned that the American who was attached to the Social Studies panel had gone home due to serious health reasons.

'That's sad, if you give me his address I'll send him a card', said Adrian.

'You don't want anything to do with him after the trouble he caused your wife!' was the surprising reply.

Adrian looked shocked – was there something I hadn't told him?

Apparently, the American had been working undercover for the CIA. When his contract with the Botswana Ministry of Education came to an end he looked around for another job so he could remain in the country. It seemed that he had put pressure on my boss to recommend that my contract was not renewed. My boss went along with it and told the ministry that I was unsuitable because I was not from Southern Africa. Once the position became vacant he recommended the American for the job. However, the ministry said that, as he had advised that my contract should not be renewed because I was an ex-pat, they were unable to employ another ex-pat in the role.

Adrian told me that his colleague was most upset about the incident, both for the stress it had caused our family and also because of the underhand nature of it.

The incident opened our eyes to an aspect of international affairs that we had been blissfully unaware of.

Although it did not stop us from trusting people, we were more careful about taking everything at face value.

As soon as we arrived at T62 everyone wanted to see the new baby.

'Ah! Neo you are welcome!' said Rosemary when she hurried to greet us, closely followed by Pinky and Tshoganetso.

When Alyrene was still very young I sometimes put her on a blanket in the garden for the girls to watch over. Sunniva and Ambijorn often joined in. Like most mothers, my ears were alert to sudden silences as well as screams. One morning I hurried outside to see Alyrene all on her own after the children had gone next door and found other games to play.

Rosemary left around that time but we kept in touch with the family. She went to live with Richard Alschner who had built himself a house in Francistown.

I asked Beauty Magula, if she knew anyone who would like to help in the house. Beauty was Melinda's Setswana teacher at John Mackenzie School. We became friends due to our mutual love of writing. Her first book 'Mma-Tshenolo and the School Teacher' won first prize in a competition and she went on to write many more.

She recommended Stella. Like Beauty, Stella's husband came from South Africa. He and Stella were dedicated to helping South African refugees in Francistown as well as supporting the work of the ANC where they could.

Stella always called Alyrene by her Setswana name, Neo, and she treated her as if she was her own special gift. She had a six year old son called Setembele who went to the local school. One day she invited Neo and I to meet her husband at their home the other side of Francistown. It was an area of small houses and rondavals packed close together. People kept a variety of livestock in their yards, especially chickens which elicited much glee from Alyrene.

Stella's husband made me feel very welcome. I realised I was in the presence of a really good man who appeared to have no bitterness for the way he had been treated in South Africa, he just wanted to make the world a better place.

Melinda was looking forward to her ninth birthday. I had been so pleased when I realised that she had been born on United Nations Day. She went to school on her birthday but came home most upset. The head teacher had taken her class for a lesson on the United Nations. He explained that it was founded after the Second World War to prevent further wars. Then he told the class about the threat of nuclear war and wrote on the blackboard: 'World War Three?' I tried not to let Melinda see how angry I was with the headmaster. Instead I told her about the Peace Movement and after a while she cheered up and had a lovely birthday party.

Elijah invited us to his farm north of Francistown. I got on well with his wife and, although his children were mainly boys, they were very friendly to our girls including Alyrene. At the end of the visit Elijah's wife gave us a live chicken which we put carefully in the back of the pickup.

It was the middle of the afternoon when we arrived on the outskirts of Francistown. Adrian suggested we went to the newly opened Thapama Hotel. We climbed up the spiral staircase and sat on the balcony overlooking the car park and hills beyond. We had just finished our drinks when we saw a chicken strutting round the car park.

After a few minutes of watching and laughing we suddenly realised where it had come from. Adrian and the girls rushed down the staircase while I took my time, carefully holding Alyrene and wondering why there wasn't a lift or even an ordinary flight of stairs. When I reached the, fortunately quiet, car park I found Adrian giving instructions to the girls on how to corner the chicken. Alyrene gave a delighted squeal and pointed as she tried to leap out of my arms and join the fun. Unbelievably we managed to catch it before anyone arrived to see what the fuss was about. On closer inspection we saw that one of the back windows of the canopy had been left slightly open.

We had another full house at Christmas. Hugh and Mmatsela came to stay and Poppy's father dropped her off unexpectedly. I was asked if I would lend Alyrene to be the baby Jesus in the manger but, after the problems the previous year when some of the participants were bitten by ants, I declined. However, Emily took part in a production of Aladdin in the school pantomime. After Christmas Michael, Nora and the children arrived on their way back from Zambia.

The New Year ushered in 1984 and much was made by media across the world of George Orwell's dire predictions.

For us it was a time of indecision. Adrian had been told that his successor would be appointed before we left so there would be time to train him in the different aspects of the job, but it was proving difficult to find someone suitable.

He was still travelling a lot and, after a visit to Gaborone, Adrian arrived home early looking flustered.

'I've been asked to stay another year, what do you think?'

I could hear Alyrene laughing in the bathroom. Although it wasn't part of Stella's job, she insisted on bathing 'Neo' every day before she went off duty. Melinda and Emily were playing outside in the sunshine.

I glanced at my type writer on the table with the next chapter of my novel waiting to be finished. Ignoring images of my mother's and mother-in-law's stricken faces that flashed into my mind, I nodded.

'Another year would give us both time to finish things here. Melinda will still be able to go to the village school and Alyrene will be old enough to join a mother and toddlers group.'

Adrian smiled with relief. 'We'll be on leave for three months this summer and then next year we'll be home for good.'

The girls and I were pleased not to be leaving our friends just yet. I had become particularly close to my Dutch friends in our women's discussion group. Carolien and her husband had adopted a baby who had been abandoned at the hospital. Her husband had been posted to Ethiopia on a short term contract but Caroline did not want to leave her teaching job at John McKenzie. They had a house in three acres of land on the edge of Francistown. Our other Dutch friends kept horses there for the boys and Melinda loved being allowed the occasional ride.

Soon after our decision to stay in Botswana for another 18 months I picked up Melinda from the riding school she attended. I knew that the teacher was leaving and selling the horses but was surprised when she asked if we would like to buy the smallest horse, Arabella.

Melinda looked at me pleadingly so, on the spur of the moment, I said yes. Adrian was away at the time and when he came home he wasn't as excited as the rest of us at having a horse. I had checked with Carolien that we could keep Arabella at her place but had not worked out the logistics of getting her there.

As it was summer, there was no water in the river and we realised that the best way to avoid traffic would be along the river bed. With Melinda sitting proudly astride a rather fractious horse, Adrian held Arabella's reins and trudged the 5 km in the heat of the day on uneven sand.

Emily, Alyrene and I, as well as Ans, Art and their boys were waiting when they finally arrived at Carolien's place. This was the beginning of friendships that lasted many years despite the distance of time and place.

Even in the short time we had lived in Botswana there had been significant changes in the surrounding countries, notably Zimbabwe.

By this time John McKenzie school had a steady stream of new pupils whose white parents had found Zimbabwe a difficult place to live. I became friendly with a woman whose daughter was in Melinda's class. She was missing the place that had been home for her entire life and was doing her best to adapt.

'It's so different here,' she said. 'Blacks can do any job they like.'

'It's their country,' I said reasonably.

She hastened to agree. 'It's just,' she paused, 'not what I'm used to. But it works well, there's no discrimination.'

It wasn't just whites who were receiving sanctuary in Botswana.

I was shocked to see lorries full of Matabele refugees from the area of Zimbabwe closest to us on their way to the camp at Dukwi, 132 km north west of Francistown.

The camp had been established by the Lutheran World Federation in 1978 to cope with the influx of refugees from Rhodesia, Namibia, Angola, South Africa and, by 1984, Matabele people from Zimbabwe. At that time the refugee camp hosted around 45,000 people.

Soon after the Easter holidays ended, Melinda said there was a new girl in her class. I asked where she came from.

'I don't know, she cries all the time.'

Later, Marie told me that she was Swedish and her father worked at Dukwi Refugee camp. Although the school at the camp had a good reputation, many of the children were traumatised from fleeing their home countries. The family were looking for somewhere in Francistown for Synnöve and her mother, Gudrun, to live but for the time being Synnöve was staying with a Swedish couple. When I met Gudrun, she told me they had previously lived in Rhodesia when her husband had been a pastor there. They had left before Zimbabwe became independent and were shocked that some of their previous parishioners were now fleeing for their lives.

I suggested to Gudrun that they could live in our house when we went on leave in June. Fortunately, a house on our road became available for them just before we returned.

Chapter 28

Planes, Boats and Trains

Like many ex-pats we decided to use our travel allowance to make a holiday of our journey home.

We flew to Frankfurt and stayed overnight with a university friend of Adrian's. The next day was a relaxing boat trip down the River Rhine from Mainz to Cologne. After spending five years in a country with no large rivers it was a joy to watch the world go by as we cruised along one of Europe's great waterways. Melinda and Emily were fascinated by the castles we passed and Alyrene waved at people in other boats. After a night at the Mondial Hotel next to Cologne cathedral we decided to visit the world famous Roman museum which had been built on the site of a 3rd-century villa. Adrian and I were impressed with the mosaics but, as the girls had no experience of museums, they could not understand what the fuss was about.

In the afternoon we took a train to Lübbecke to stay with Friedel and Eberhard. They were as friendly as when we had last seen them in Francistown and Tabo was excited to have Melinda and Emily to play with. Friedel was interested in hearing news about the Women's Discussion group and said that she had joined a local women's group. I was fascinated to see an old-fashioned loom in an attic room and she showed me some of the things she had woven. However, I was unable to see the sights of this ancient riverside town as I spent the two days in bed suffering from flu or exhaustion.

We were looking forward to seeing Wolfgang the next day in Hamelin. I had decided not to tell the girls the story of the Pied Piper as I found it rather disturbing so they were surprised when Wolfgang solemnly told them that if they heard a flute playing they were not to follow it. Despite the rain, we could see that it was a beautiful town full of medieval buildings with preservation orders on them.

Wolfgang lived with his parents in a farmhouse on the edge of Hamelin. Despite the language barrier they were most welcoming. When his mother realised that Wolfgang had seen Alyrene when she was only a few hours old she assumed the role of Grandmother for our overnight visit.

She also told me, with Wolfgang interpreting, that she wanted Wolfgang to settle down and stay in Germany. She described how she and her husband had arrived in this part of Germany in the Second World War. They had previously farmed near the eastern border and had just managed to escape the advancing Russian army by putting a few possessions in a hand cart and fleeing to safety in the west of Germany.

Feeling refreshed, we enjoyed looking round the Palace Gardens in Hanover with Wolfgang the next day before catching our train to Hamburg. From there we took an overnight train to Stockholm.

This twelve hour journey involved the train travelling by boat to take us across the Baltic Sea. Although it was June, there was snow when we arrived in Stockholm. We were pleased that we had asked Air Botswana to make a reservation for a room for the day at an international hotel. After a night in a three berth sleeper we were looking forward to getting tidied up before travelling to Lars and his family in Umeå.

We were cold and wet when we arrived at the hotel in an assortment of anoraks, rucksacks, two disgruntled children and a baby. I went confidently to the desk and said we had a reservation. The smartly dressed receptionist looked me up and down, skimmed the register and informed us no such reservation had been made. At that point I caught site of myself in a mirror and vowed that I would never again walk into a hotel looking like that. Money talks and we looked penniless. However we found another hotel and, after a rest, had an enjoyable boat trip around the archipelago.

The eight hour train journey north from Stockholm to Umeå passed without mishap. The city is situated on the bank of the Umeå River near the Gulf of Bothnia. Lars, who worked at the University, was keen to hear Adrian's news about the projects they had both been involved in. He showed us round the town which is also known as the City of Birches due to the hundreds of birch trees that line the avenues. Despite the cold, we enjoyed walking along tree-lined paths in the evening when, unlike Botswana, it was still light. Emily was unwell for the first two days but recovered to celebrate her seventh birthday and we went berry picking in a nearby forest. Unfortunately Adrian was ill during our last couple of days. Gunilla was working so Lars took their son, Ole, myself and the girls to see salmon on their migration route from the Baltic Sea to a river that passed through Umeå. It was fascinating watching them leaping over obstacles as they made their way upstream to spawn.

We continued our journey by train and, by the time we got to Norway, the weather had turned sunny. Our seats were near the restaurant car and, as I looked at the beautiful scenery, Alyrene crawled along the floor until one of the chefs picked her up and took her to the kitchen. When I went to see what was going on I found her the centre of attention as she sat on a table watching the cooks at work.

We stayed overnight in Trondheim before continuing to Oslo. Elisabeth, Sven and Karen-Kristine met us and we drove along the coast, then inland to their house which was on a wooded hillside overlooking a lake. The next day was hot and we relaxed by the lake. Later Sven took us to another lake which was a crystal clear deep blue. When I commented how pretty it was, he told us that it was because of acid rain from Britain and the lake was dead. After a good night's sleep we moved to their holiday home on a fiord near Arendal and spent the rest of the week swimming, fishing, sunbathing and exploring the area in their little boat.

We had planned to spend our last night near the airport in Stavanger but Sven insisted on driving us there. The sun was up by 4,30 am and we drove through more beautiful scenery. An official at the airport looked at our passports and couldn't understand how we had got from Frankfurt to

Stavanger. I had been mildly disappointed that our passports hadn't been stamped along the way but hadn't realised that the lack of official stamps would cause a problem. It was fortunate that Sven had remained with us while we were being cross examined at immigration control. He explained that we had travelled by train and our passports had not been asked for. The officer shook his head at the lack of efficiency of the railways and, after a few more probing questions, we were free to go.

Our arrival wasn't as exciting as the previous year. Family and friends were pleased to see us but understandably everyone was busy with their daily lives. Melinda was still on the school roll so she and Emily spent the last three weeks of the summer term at the village school. The school sports day was an opportunity to meet other parents and Adrian joined in the fathers' race.

We were shocked to find wallpaper hanging off some of our walls where the 'damp proofing' had been done. Adrian was able to sort out the problem but it made us realise that, unlike our life in Botswana, leisure time 'back home' was often spent on house and garden maintenance. I was pleased that, unlike some of my friends in Botswana, I had done the cooking and dish-washing at weekends so I hadn't lost touch with the realities of life.

It was good spending time with Adrian's parents in the next village and mine in Somerset. On our way to my parents we called on George and Heather in Oakham. We enjoyed seeing them and Alistair again as well as meeting Euan who was just two months younger than Alyrene.

We also spent a week on a narrow boat with Jill, Dave and their children. We went from Upton on Seven to Stratford on Avon. When I heard Melinda say loudly 'Who is this Shakespeare person?' I was glad that we had this opportunity to introduce the children to some of our cultural heritage. Alyrene had already turned one but we had discouraged her from walking before the holiday as we didn't want her to fall over the side of the boat.

Alyrene continued to crawl everywhere until we arrived at Heathrow for our plane to Botswana. Ines and Tony Russell and their boys came to see us at the airport which was particularly busy. Alyrene chose that moment to show that she could walk. She toddled into the crowd and was almost out of sight by the time we caught up with her.

Chapter 29

Journalism, Swaziland, Tsodilo Hills and South African Raid

It felt good to be back in Francistown and we were determined to make the most of our last year.

Adrian was pleased to find things running smoothly at TAPU but disappointed that a successor had not been appointed to work alongside him. He was straight back into making regular trips to Gaborone and running courses throughout the country.

School was still on holiday which gave Melinda and Emily a week to settle down. Arabella had been well looked after and Melinda enjoyed riding again. Both girls were ready to go back to school the following week and their teachers were interested in their holiday diaries and asked them to read them to the class.

Stella was pleased to see us and said how much she had missed Neo. She made sure that Alyrene stayed away from me in the morning when I was at my desk in the bedroom writing.

Emily was disappointed there were no ballet lessons this term. However, she and her friends enjoyed producing their own dance routines and plays.

I also had the opportunity to be in a play. It was twenty years since I had done any acting and I was excited, although nervous, to be involved again. Jonathon, an Englishman, was directing Tom Stoppard's one act play, The Real Inspector Hound. Melinda and Emily wanted to know all about the play but, as the plot is quite absurd it was difficult to explain. They were slightly upset that I was playing the part of Mrs Drudge, the maid, and asked if I would rather play Lady Muldoon.

'Not really, she has to kiss several people,' I said conspiratorially and they agreed that wouldn't be good in front of an audience!

As it was only a month from the first rehearsal to performance, Adrian did not arrange any overnight trips so that he could look after the girls in the evenings.

The play was performed outside at the Marang Hotel and the final rehearsals were fraught. There was a power cut in the middle of the rehearsal on Monday, the scenery blew down in a high wind on Tuesday and the settee collapsed on Wednesday's dress rehearsal.

Adrian came to Friday's performance. He brought the girls and Jason, who was staying with us, as well as Stella and Beauty Magula. He said it was quite funny sitting next to the smartly dressed lady who works in his house and looking at his wife on stage wearing hair rollers and Stella's overall.

The play was a great success. Although it was my last foray into amateur dramatics, I continued to enjoy theatre productions especially when Emily and Alyrene played parts at the Broadbent Theatre when we were living in Lincolnshire.

Soon afterwards I took Emily to the Marang to hear the Story of Baba and the Little Elephant. It was part of an event organised by the Francistown music society. While we were there I met John Kula, the Botswana Guardian's resident reporter in Francistown. He asked if I would like to write a review of the evening. I was, of course, delighted and my Concert Review appeared on 12th October. John then asked if I would like regular work on a freelance basis. Soon afterwards I received a phone call from the Editor offering me a job as a reporter of social events in Francistown for the equivalent of £50 per month. I was over the moon, especially when I received my official press card. I had no problem in finding things to write about but had to decline when the Editor asked me to report on a football match. He quite understood when I phoned to explain that I was only five feet tall and knew nothing about football. Instead he sent me to investigate The Cave, a night club discotheque and restaurant that had just opened. I asked Carolien to go with me and we sat in a corner watching people who were apparently having a great time in the small dark space. The manager was delighted to show us round and he was probably as pleased as I was to see my half page report in the next issue of the Guardian. I was also encouraged to choose my own topics, one I particularly enjoyed writing was a three quarter page spread with photographs on Parks and Gardens in Francistown. The article I was most proud of was The Two Faces of Ford. I was asked to go to the Francistown branch of Kalahari Ford when their showroom received the only Ford Sierra XRB in Botswana. It was with great satisfaction that I read the full article in the next edition of the Botswana Guardian, Botswana's first independent newspaper.

Ans and Ad had moved to Swaziland and they invited us to spend Christmas and New Year with them. Melinda and Emily were anxious about spending Christmas away from home but we bought a small Christmas tree and opened our presents from England before we left. I was touched by Melinda's message on her present to me: 'I hope when you go reporting you will put this nice powder on because it smells so nice.'

We went via Pretoria and stayed overnight with Gill who had moved there with her South African partner and 15 month old baby boy.

The drive from Pretoria took four and a half hours. I had no idea what to expect, except that Swaziland was a small country mainly surrounded by South Africa and with Mozambique on its eastern border. As we climbed high into the Drakensburg Mountains our road wound past ancient rock formations with vistas of hills and verdant valleys in the distance.

Mbabane, the capital, was close to the border. It was situated in a valley but Ans and Ad lived half way up the valley side with spectacular views. Their carpet selling business was in an airy premises in the town centre. Adje and Mark were pleased to see the girls and most of the time they all got on well.

'We thought you'd like to help decorate the Christmas tree,' Ans suggested the day after we arrived.

'It's a big one,' said Melinda approvingly.

They were keen to take us to one of their favourite spots a short drive out of town to a shallow but fast flowing stream. We took a picnic and settled on the bank to watch the children skimming down what the boys called the 'fooffy slide.' This entailed sliding down some flat rocks covered with an inch of water in the middle of the stream.

Another day we went to a spa with a large swimming pool. While the children leapt in and out of the pool, I had a spa treatment and came out feeling refreshed.

'Boring!' complained the boys when their parents announced we would have a trip round Swaziland. However, as the country is so small it only took half a day. We drove past acres of sugar cane until we came to Piggs Peak which was originally a gold mining area and has since become important for forestry.

Everyone was excited about going to a drive-in movie on New Year's Eve especially having take-away food to eat as we watched the film. However, the boys were bursting with energy after sitting in the car so when we came home, with some help from Adrian and Ad, they took the Christmas tree down and set fire to it outside!

Despite the chaos surrounding us, Ans and I found time to catch up on news about mutual friends.

She shook her head when I asked if there were any women's groups in Mbabane.

'Ad and I run the business together so I'm too busy. We are getting to know people at the Rotary Club but it's not the same.'

'Do you have any time to yourself?'

Ans nodded then said quietly, 'I write poetry.'

'That's fantastic.'

I knew not to say any more but was touched when, later, she handed me a folder of her poems. I was even more touched when I saw that one of them had been written for me.

We felt refreshed after our holiday but Adrian was worried that there was still no sign of his successor. He was confident in Elijah's ability to run the printing department and Innocent's to run the carpentry but, with no one in overall command, their jobs would be difficult. He hoped to arrange more training for them in England when we returned.

I felt it was time for Alyrene to be with children her own age so I enrolled her at Chris Corker's nursery. Stella enjoyed taking her there at nine o'clock and fetching her at noon which meant they had the afternoon together which they both enjoyed. It also gave me time to meet people and write up reports. When I first started working for the Botswana Guardian I used to deliver my copy to the guard on the night train and someone from the office would pick it up when the train arrived in Gaborone the next morning. Then I heard that telex had arrived in Francistown. It was much easier to drop my copy at the office of a friend who would then telex it direct to the Guardian office.

Life continued to be hectic with the girls' activities, friends in crisis, saying hello and goodbye as well as doing our jobs. Emily was particularly affected at saying goodbye to Ambijörn. The Vikings left on the morning train and about fifteen of us gathered at the station to see them off. When they got on the train Emily rushed down the platform screaming 'Ambijörn!' Adrian ran after her and lifted her near the carriage window; when I glanced round I saw that we were all sniffing into our handkerchiefs.

I was looking forward to being 40 in April with some trepidation. Unfortunately Adrian had left for a two week teachers' course the day before my birthday. This trip involved travelling with 30 teachers to learn about the flora, fauna and geography of Ngamiland which encompassed Maun and the North West of Botswana. Adrian suggested I came with the girls for the end of the course.

Although Melinda and Emily were sensible I didn't really want them to be responsible for Alyrene on the 500 km drive. The obvious solution was to ask Stella to come too. She agreed on the understanding that she could bring her little boy as well. We had finally got a telephone so I phoned Adrian to say what we were doing and he said he would sort out suitable accommodation.

By this time I was writing for the Northern Advertiser as well as the Guardian so I decided to stop in Nata and interview the owners of the newly established Nata Lodge. It was an ideal place to stop after the two hour drive from Francistown. The next stop was Gweta Rest Camp situated near the Makgadikgadi Pans game reserve.

We stayed longer than I had intended and the sun was shining in my eyes as I continued west. We arrived on the outskirts of Maun at about five o'clock. I drove carefully on the dirt road, past traders and children playing until a dog suddenly ran into the middle of the road. Throughout my time on African roads it had been drummed into me not to slam on the breaks, even if there was a small animal on the road. I knew that, if I swerved I was in danger of hitting someone.

'Well done, Madam,' said Stella above the children's gasps as I slowed but kept to the middle of road and hit the dog. My heart was pounding as I steered a steady course to the teachers' centre in Maun.

It was the first time I had been there since Wolfgang left and I missed his concern for myself and the girls. The German who had taken his place couldn't quite understand why we were there. However, our accommodation near the river in the house of a very pleasant ex-pat woman was lovely. There was a slight problem when I realised she hadn't been told about Stella and Setembile but she soon sorted it out and they stayed with her maid who had pleasant quarters on the property.

'Mum kill dog,' said Alyrene gleefully when Adrian asked about our journey.

Adrian was shocked but Melinda told him I had done it to avoid children playing in the road.

'Where did you all stay?' I asked to change the subject.

'We camped in tents along the way. We went as far as the Namibian border. The teachers couldn't believe how remote it was. Until we reached Mohembo there were no villages, just a few settlements with huts made mainly of grass.'

'Did you see the caves?'

'Yes, the stalactites and stalagmites at Gcwihaba are amazing. But we had to pass under thousands of bats hanging upside down from the cave ceiling.'

'Weren't you afraid they would jump on you?' Emily screwed up her face at the thought.

'Not really, we were more afraid of the hyenas.' Adrian laughed, then seeing the horror on the girls' faces, he explained that Hyena's Lair was the name given to the caves by the San people several thousand years ago but the hyenas were long gone.

He went on to describe the caves and a frozen waterfall of rock.

'I took some photos but I don't know how well they'll come out.'

Melinda asked if he was frightened in the dark.

He explained that they had taken their generator to the cave entrance and rigged up some flood lights so they were able to see quite a lot. When they explored further into the cave they used torches.

'Were the Tsodilo Hills far from there?' I asked.

'Yes, another three hour journey. The rock paintings were incredible.'

'Do you remember the rock paintings at the Matopos?' I asked the girls.'

'Where we danced like the bushman,' said Emily.

'There are far more paintings at Tsodilo. The people who made them think that Tsodilo is where life began.' Adrian was quiet as he reflected on what he had seen.

Later I asked if he thought the area was as remote as the Kalahari.

'I think it's more remote. The Kalahari is in the middle of Botswana and, even though they aren't tarmac, the roads are well defined and there are villages along the route.'

Stella and Setembele enjoyed their time in Maun with us. As we got in the vehicle to drive back to Francistown I wondered if I would ever have the opportunity to return.

Adrian's contract didn't finish until the end of September but we decided that I would go home earlier with the girls. We wanted them to begin school at the beginning of term and I needed to look for a job. However, what I really wanted to do was start a language school for Europeans going to work in Africa.

As the time of our departure neared we were all increasingly fidgety. June 14th was Emily's eighth birthday and we were shocked to hear that the South African Defence Force had invaded Botswana in the early hours of the morning. The Botswana Guardian's account of the raid, in which 12 people died, asked challenging questions. It seemed that a lot of the shooting was indiscriminate. I continued to send in local news while keenly following reports of the aftermath of the raid by journalists including Mxolisi Mgxahe who was originally from South Africa.

I slowly filled our large trunk that had been made at TAPU with things we had accumulated over the years. The trunk was going from Francistown as unaccompanied luggage and took several of Adrian's colleagues to lift it into the TAPU truck. They all wanted to see it leave on its journey to England so they jumped into the truck and I followed in our car with the girls.

'Will our things be safe?' asked Melinda anxiously as we watched it being loaded onto the plane.

'Of course,' I said, quickly banishing my own similar thoughts. 'It will be waiting for us at Humberside.'

The rest of our time passed in a blur as we said goodbye to friends and acquaintances with promises to meet again.

We left Francistown on July 11th, Alyrene's second birthday. I had invited a few friends for a lunch time birthday and departure party. Stella was particularly sad to say goodbye and I was pleased that she was going to work for Chris Corker at her nursery school.

Joe Butali came to see us at our hotel in Gaborone. The girls found it hard to understand why he wasn't his usual happy self but he really wanted to talk about the South African raid that he had witnessed. It made a great impression on all of us.

We were subdued when we said our final goodbyes to Adrian. The girls waved franticly, then we walked out of sight.

As we waited in the small departure area I noticed Mxolisi Mgxahe standing rigidly against a wall. The Botswana Government, probably with pressure from South Africa, was deporting the journalist to Sweden due to his detailed reporting of the raid. My heart went out to him, I was returning to my own country but he was leaving the country he had called home for a far off destination.

We were traveling via Kenya and, for the first part of the journey the plane was only half full. The girls settled down and I thought about the things we had done during the last six years and, just as important, the friends we had made. I was comforted as I thought about Ans's poem at the bottom of my bag.

Where is my friend who looked at this world,
The dark and the light, with questioning eye
And lived both sides of night and day, balancing carefully
In a personal way the joy and the pain.
I miss this friend that in the darkness saw stars,
In sunlight the shadow's glare and mixed them fresh
With a humorous mind, searching a pattern worth living for.

Flash Forward

Thirty five years later Melinda was living in New Zealand with her family. She and her daughter, Maya, were walking on a remote beach when they fell into conversation with a man who had originally lived in South Africa. When Melinda said she had lived in Botswana when she was a child he went quiet and seemed upset, then told her that he was one of the soldiers who had been ordered to take part in the raid and had felt haunted by it ever since.

Chapter 30

Re-entry and Return

The summer of 1985 was one of the coldest on record. The average July temperature in the English Midlands that year was 16°C and in August it dropped to 14°C. Although it was winter in Botswana, the temperature in Francistown was a comfortable 18°C when we left.

I was pleased to be back in our house with our own furniture but had forgotten how small it was. It seemed even smaller when Adrian's brother, David, arrived with from Canada with Alexandra and Amy who were the same ages as Melinda and Emily. Space became even more of a problem when Granny and Papa visited, which they did often as they were delighted to be re-united with five of their granddaughters.

It was rather a strange time. David and his wife, Gerry, were separated and he wasn't used to looking after his daughters on a regular basis. I had got used to having someone to cook and keep the house clean for the last six years and the girls were used to the freedom of playing outside with their friends.

They were excited when I suggested a trip to the seaside at Skegness. I had forgotten how far it was and how the east wind whipped across the beach. Alyrene was desperate to follow the older girls as they splashed in the sea but she clung to me, shivering, when she got wet. After they had dried themselves with towels they had dropped in the sand we took them to the nearest café. I used to be proud of the way Melinda and Emily behaved when we went out but they seemed to have left their manners in Botswana.

When our chest of luggage arrived I didn't know where to put everything.

'What shall I do?' I asked my brother-in-law.'

'Move to a bigger house,' he said.

'We must get jobs first,' I sighed. 'And a childminder for Alyrene.'

I asked Angela if she knew of anyone in the village who would be suitable and she suggested her next door neighbour.

Leaving David to look after the children who were running round like wild things, I went to the large detached house over the road. Unlike our house with no front garden, Ivy House was set back from the road with a large rose bed on the lawn in front of the house. I walked up the drive and knocked.

Mrs Coe was a pleasant woman and I felt Alyrene would be in safe hands but she explained that she planned to move to a smaller property in Market Rasen. I caught my breath, it was just the sort of house Adrian and I had dreamed of. As I stood on the doorstep I glanced at the spacious back garden.

'Would you like to see the garden?' she asked.

'I'd love to.'

I followed her up the path by a hedge that divided the lawn from a large overgrown vegetable area. At the bottom of the garden was a garage and behind that an orchard. We stopped at the gate to a field that sloped down to a pond.

'Who owns the field?' I asked.

'We do, it's a real bother having to cut all that grass with a lawn mower.'

'Do you keep animals on it?' I pictured Melinda cantering round the field on Arabella.

'Mrs Coe shook her head, 'Not since the children left.'

As we walked back I looked up at the windows. There were five bedrooms; maybe one could be used to teach international students. Then I forced myself back to the reality of our finances.

'It's lovely, we need a bigger house but I hadn't realised you had so much land as well.'

'It's too much trouble,' she said. 'There are the hedges to trim and each year we have to contribute to cleaning the beck at the bottom of the field.

I knew that beck was the Lincolnshire word for a particular type of stream. After spending six years living in drought conditions, the idea of a stream at the bottom of the garden was most appealing.

As I thanked Mrs Coe she told me the name of her estate agent and that she had told them she didn't want a 'For Sale' sign outside unless it was really necessary.

That evening I phoned Adrian. After chatting about how we were, I mentioned that Ivy House was for sale.

'Buy it!' he said.

The rest of that cold summer passed in a blur. After David and the girls left I drove to my parents in Somerset. I had been a confident driver on bush roads, but had no recent experience of roundabouts. By the time we were half way the girls were bored and I was looking for somewhere to stop. However, I hadn't intended to stop on a roundabout as I bumped into the car in front. The driver got out looking angry but, when he was confronted with three crying children and their quivering mother, he took charge. Fortunately his car was driveable and the AA arrived soon afterwards to sort us out.

It was a great relief when Adrian came home, although I wasn't happy when he said he had to return at Easter to help Mogae Mokwathi who had taken over from him at TAPU just before he left. However, that was in the future and our immediate problem was to get work, especially as we were about to put our house on the market prior to making an offer on Ivy House. Adrian took a job selling double glazing and I went into market research. Both jobs entailed knocking on people's doors throughout West Lindsey and Grimsby. It was an interesting way of getting in touch with life in Lincolnshire but we knew that the remuneration wouldn't be enough to pay the mortgage on Ivy House so Adrian took a full time teaching post at the secondary school near the RAF station at Coningsby. I was still intent on starting a language school and so worked as a supply teacher which gave me flexibility.

Melinda and Emily settled back at the primary school. I found a childminder who was prepared to have Alyrene on the days I worked and did not charge for the other days. Alyrene adored Patty and she always called to see her after we left Lincolnshire many years later.

The girls enjoyed watching Christmas shows on television but it did not make up for the midsummer Christmases and parties they had been used to. There was a feeling that we couldn't really settle down until we moved to our new house.

We had a week between buying Ivy House and leaving our current home. This gave us the February half term to trundle our possessions across the road, helped by a farmer friend with a tractor and trailer. We continued to be dogged by bad weather; it was the coldest winter since January 1963, with an average temperature of 1°C. The central heating system had seen better days and the wind whipped through cracks and crevices.

I also noticed a drop in temperature from some of the Osgodby residents.

'I didn't know Ivy House was for sale,' a couple of people said as if there had been some skulduggery going on.

Melinda settled down well once she discovered that she could see her friend Rosemary's bedroom from hers and they set up a messaging system.

Emily didn't settle so easily. She felt the cold badly and we had several trips to the doctor but he could find nothing wrong.

As Easter drew nearer I wondered how we would cope in our new, but cold house when Adrian was in Francistown.

On the spur of the moment I picked up the phone. 'Are you doing anything at Easter?' I asked as I heard the familiar voice of Nils Viking.

'I think we're inviting the Rossers to stay!' he said.

We booked our flight to Sweden for the same day as Adrian was leaving for Botswana. Nils met us at the airport and drove us to their home in Svatmangatan, a few kilometres outside Stockholm. There was snow on the ground but, soon after we arrived, the four older children ran outside, kicked off their shoes and sat down busily making things in the snow.

'They've never done that before.' Marie looked out in amazement.

I stood by the window to get a closer look. 'They're playing the same games they played in our garden in Botswana.'

'But they never take their shoes off outside!' said Nils.

'They did in Botswana, and now they're together they are mentally back there.'

We shook our heads as we realised the enormous impact that living in Botswana had made on all their lives.

'How are they settling in at school?' I asked.

''It was difficult for Sunniva at first, she had forgotten some of her Swedish. How has it been for Melinda and Emily?' asked Marie.

'Ok for Melinda but Emily is finding it difficult. I've been told that eight is a difficult age for children to have a big change in their life. How was it for Ambijörn?

'He was okay, I think it helped that children here don't start school till they are seven.'

'And what about you?'

Nils shrugged. 'My job's okay but Marie is still looking.'

After a while four wet but happy children ran into the house.

Easter was early that year and the children enjoyed looking for eggs hidden in the snow. The next day we went to a large department store in Stockholm which had two escalators.

'Come!' said Sunniva and Ambijörn as they jumped on the nearest.

Melinda and Emily followed warily as they had no recollection of seeing one before.

At the top of the escalator was a magnificently carved Dala Horse. Its red body and brightly coloured painted harness have made it an unofficial national symbol and we came home with several tiny Dala Horses which are still a reminder of our time in Sweden.

From Stockholm we went north to visit Gudrun, Eric and Synnöve Zachrisson in Orsa.

Marie came with us to the railway station. We waited on a bench while she checked that the train was running to schedule.

'What bad luck,' she said, and told us there was a problem with our five hour train journey to Orsa in central Sweden.

'We'll be fine,' I said as the children waved frantic goodbyes.

Alyrene was asleep when we had to leave the train and transfer to a coach. In the confusion we left her Peepo book on the train. We drove past forests and small towns until we got back on a train at another railway station. It was cold and almost dark when we reached Orsa but there was warm welcome from Gudrun and Synnöve at the station.

We drove though the town centre and past the beautiful White Church where Erick was the präst or pastor. On either side of the narrow road to their home were silver birch trees, their white trunks rising out of the snow. The prästerhus was a large red-brick house surrounded by tall conifer trees.

I was exhausted by this time but felt able to relax with Gudrun. Synnöve was pleased to be back in Sweden and enjoyed sledging with Melinda and Emily as well introducing them to cross country skiing.

We arrived back in Osgodby two days before Adrian returned. The cold weather continued, but we had plenty to do getting Ivy House ready for summer visitors including Ans and family from Swaziland and Carolien Venema from Botswana. Caroline and Jason where also regular visitors now they were settled in England.

By the following year we felt ready to embrace the rural life and bought some sheep from a farmer friend. Emily expressed an interest in bee keeping and she enjoyed helping Adrian when he bought some hives which he put in the orchard.

The month before Christmas 1987 I attended a diploma course in Teaching English for Specific Purposes so that I would be well qualified to set up my school specialising in English for Europeans working in Africa and Asia.

The same year, the Vikings came to England for Nil's work and it was good to return the hospitality they had given us in Sweden.

The next 15 years were busy for all of us. Wold School of English generally operated from an upstairs room in Ivy House with students staying with local families. By this time Adrian was teaching at the comprehensive school in Market Rasen and I hired classrooms there for groups of French students in the summer holidays. I continued to write and had articles published regularly in the Lincoln Business Magazine.

In 2001 Adrian accompanied a group of 16 year old students to a school in Namibia organised by World Challenge. They worked with some of the Namibian students building playground equipment. At the end of the trip Adrian went briefly to Botswana. He was pleased to see TAPU was still operating and most of the staff he had worked with were still there.

By 2001 our girls had flown the nest. Melinda did an MSc in Community Water Supply and had recently returned from working in Guatemala. Emily was working for Macmillan Publishing Company in Oxford. Alyrene joined her for a gap year and worked as a photographer before going to university. We decided it was time for us to fly away too. Adrian got a job in Oxford teaching vulnerable boys and I taught English to Speakers of Other Languages at a local college.

In 2005 Emily and Ian, who she later married, decided to take a break from their demanding jobs. Ian had previously worked for Macmillan Education in several African countries as well as Project Trust in the Bantustan of Transkei in South Africa and Emily was keen to re-visit Botswana. They asked us to join them for that part of their trip.

The way of planning holidays had changed dramatically and we booked our tickets online to Johannesburg via Switzerland because Swiss Air offered the best deal. However their staff training seemed to have neglected how to deal with on-line bookings and we, along with 20 other passengers, were stranded in Zurich for two days. We were given hotel accommodation and enough money to make the most of our enforced stopover so we enjoyed a boat trip on Lake Zurich and a visit by coach and cable car to Mount Titlis in the Alps.

Sadly our two day delay gave us no time to visit Gill in Pretoria or Jake Swartland and his wife in Gaborone.

Emily and Ian had already arrived in Mochudi and were settled into Mmatsela and Hugh's guest cottage in their garden. Time rolled back as we bumped along in Hugh's bakki to inspect their cattle at the lands. It was also good to meet Tanasa again and Veronica with her family who were living in Gaborone. The gates were closed when we went to look at our old house but the garden was well cared for and just as we remembered it.

Cameras at the ready, we arrived at the Tropic of Capricorn only to find the sign had been taken by trophy hunters. It was 25 years since Theo Riggs found us looking for somewhere to camp and told us to follow him to his farm calling, 'Put the kettle on Verna, we've got company!' Sadly Theo had died a few years previously but we had an enthusiastic welcome from Verna and her daughter, Pam. They lent us a 4x4 for bush driving and Emily and Ian camped in our old place by the River Limpopo.

Adrian, Heather and Emily at T62

Return to T62 Francistown

Our next stop was Francistown. Chris had given up the children's nursery and she and Lance had moved to a plot of land by the river. Francistown was the high point of the trip for Emily who had happy memories of T62 and the friends she had made.

We were pleased to see that TAPU was still thriving; Elijah, Innocent and Melody all remembered Emily.

We celebrated our 35th wedding anniversary at Nata Lodge on the edge of Makadagadi Pan. At dawn the next day we took a tour into the pan. It was worth braving the winter cold to see a flock of pink flamingos walking delicately on long thin legs before fluttering their red-tipped wings and flying low over the water.

Our next stop was Discovery Lodge at Maun where we spent an enjoyable day meandering through the swamps by dug-out canoe. It was another early start the following day when we joined an overnight safari tour of Moremi Game Reserve. Our guides were excellent but warned us not to leave our tents at night. As we lay in our comfortable safari tents we could hear elephants tramping through the bush, lions roaring and a hyena howling.

On our last night in Botswana we invited our TAPU friends and their children, now young adults, for drinks at the Marang Hotel. It was a fitting end to our time in Botswana.

We were looking forward to visiting Ans and family in Swaziland (renamed eSwatini in 2018) with mixed feelings. Sadly, Mark had died in a tragic accident in his early twenties. However, they were all pleased to see us as we brought back memories of happier times. Emily and Ian stayed with Adje at his farm on the outskirts of Mbabane and he enjoyed taking them to meet his friends. We were impressed by his farm but he said that he sometimes missed the wide open spaces of Botswana.

Seventeen days after meeting up with Emily and Ian in Mochudi we waved goodbye as they got the backpackers bus from Swaziland to Durban. From there they went to Cape Town before travelling to Australasia then India.

We stayed overnight in Johannesburg and visited a world heritage site within easy driving distance from the airport. The region is called the Cradle of Humankind because of the fossilized remains of hominids, animal bones and stone tools dating back approximately four million years. I was disappointed I wasn't able to go on a short tour of the Sterkfontein Caves with Adrian but I was waiting for a hip replacement and there were warnings about the number of steps and narrow pathways.

As I sat looking out at the ancient landscape I reflected on the 20 years since I was last in Africa. Our parents were no longer with us, but we had memories of our shared experiences with them. I looked at the magnificent landscape and wondered what lay ahead for us in this ever changing world of ours.

One thing was certain; we and our children would always hold a piece of Africa in our hearts.

Lightning Source UK Ltd.
Milton Keynes UK
UKHW012109280122
397857UK00001B/60